HMH SCIENCE DIMENSIONS™

Kindergarten

This Write-In Book belongs to

____

Teacher/Room

____

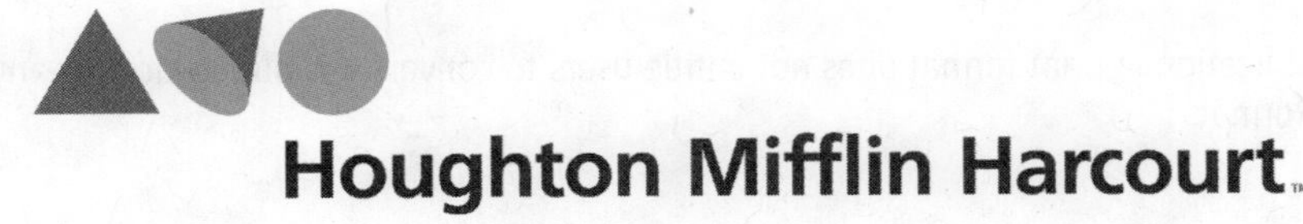

Consulting Authors

Michael A. DiSpezio
Global Educator
North Falmouth, Massachusetts

Marjorie Frank
Science Writer and Content-Area Reading Specialist
Brooklyn, New York

Michael R. Heithaus, PhD
Dean, College of Arts, Sciences & Education
Professor, Department of Biological Sciences
Florida International University
Miami, Florida

Cary Sneider, PhD
Associate Research Professor
Portland State University
Portland, Oregon

All images ©Houghton Mifflin Harcourt, Inc., unless otherwise noted

Front cover: ©HMH

Back cover: *wind socks* ©takenobu/Getty Images

Printed in the U.S.A.

ISBN 978-0-544-71323-9

7 8 9 10 0877 25 24 23 22 21 20 19 18 17

4500661292 B C D E F G

Program Advisors

Paul D. Asimow, PhD
Eleanor and John R. McMillan Professor of Geology and Geochemistry
California Institute of Technology
Pasadena, California

Eileen Cashman, PhD
Professor
Humboldt State University
Arcata, California

Mark B. Moldwin, PhD
Professor of Space Sciences and Engineering
University of Michigan
Ann Arbor, Michigan

Kelly Y. Neiles, PhD
Assistant Professor of Chemistry
St. Mary's College of Maryland
St. Mary's City, Maryland

Sten Odenwald, PhD
Astronomer
NASA Goddard Spaceflight Center
Greenbelt, Maryland

Bruce W. Schafer
Director of K-12 STEM Collaborations, retired
Oregon University System
Portland, Oregon

Barry A. Van Deman
President and CEO
Museum of Life and Science
Durham, North Carolina

Kim Withers, PhD
Assistant Professor
Texas A&M University-Corpus Christi
Corpus Christi, Texas

Adam D. Woods, PhD
Professor
California State University, Fullerton
Fullerton, California

Classroom Reviewers

Michelle Barnett
Lichen K-8 School
Citrus Heights, California

Brandi Bazarnik
Skycrest Elementary
Citrus Heights, California

Kristin Wojes-Broetzmann
Saint Anthony Parish School
Menomonee Falls, Wisconsin

Andrea Brown
District Science and STEAM Curriculum TOSA
Hacienda La Puente Unified School District
Hacienda Heights, California

Denice Gayner
Earl LeGette Elementary
Fair Oaks, California

Emily Giles
Elementary Curriculum Consultant
Kenton County School District
Ft. Wright, Kentucky

Crystal Hintzman
Director of Curriculum, Instruction and Assessment
School District of Superior
Superior, Wisconsin

Roya Hosseini
Junction Avenue K-8 School
Livermore, California

Cynthia Alexander Kirk
Classroom Teacher, Learning Specialist
West Creek Academy
Valencia, California

Marie LaCross
Fair Oaks Ranch Community School
Santa Clarita, California

Emily Miller
Science Specialist
Madison Metropolitan School District
Madison, Wisconsin

Monica Murray, EdD
Principal
Bassett Unified School District
La Puente, California

Wendy Savaske
Director of Instructional Services
School District of Holmen
Holmen, Wisconsin

Tina Topoleski
District Science Supervisor
Jackson School District
Jackson, New Jersey

You are a scientist.

You are naturally curious.

You may have wondered things such as these.

Why does ice melt?

Why does your heart beat?

Where does thunder come from?

What do animals need to grow?

HMH SCIENCE **DIMENSIONS**™
will SPARK your curiosity.

Where do you see yourself when you grow up?

Draw what you want to do when you grow up.

Be a scientist.
Work like real scientists work.

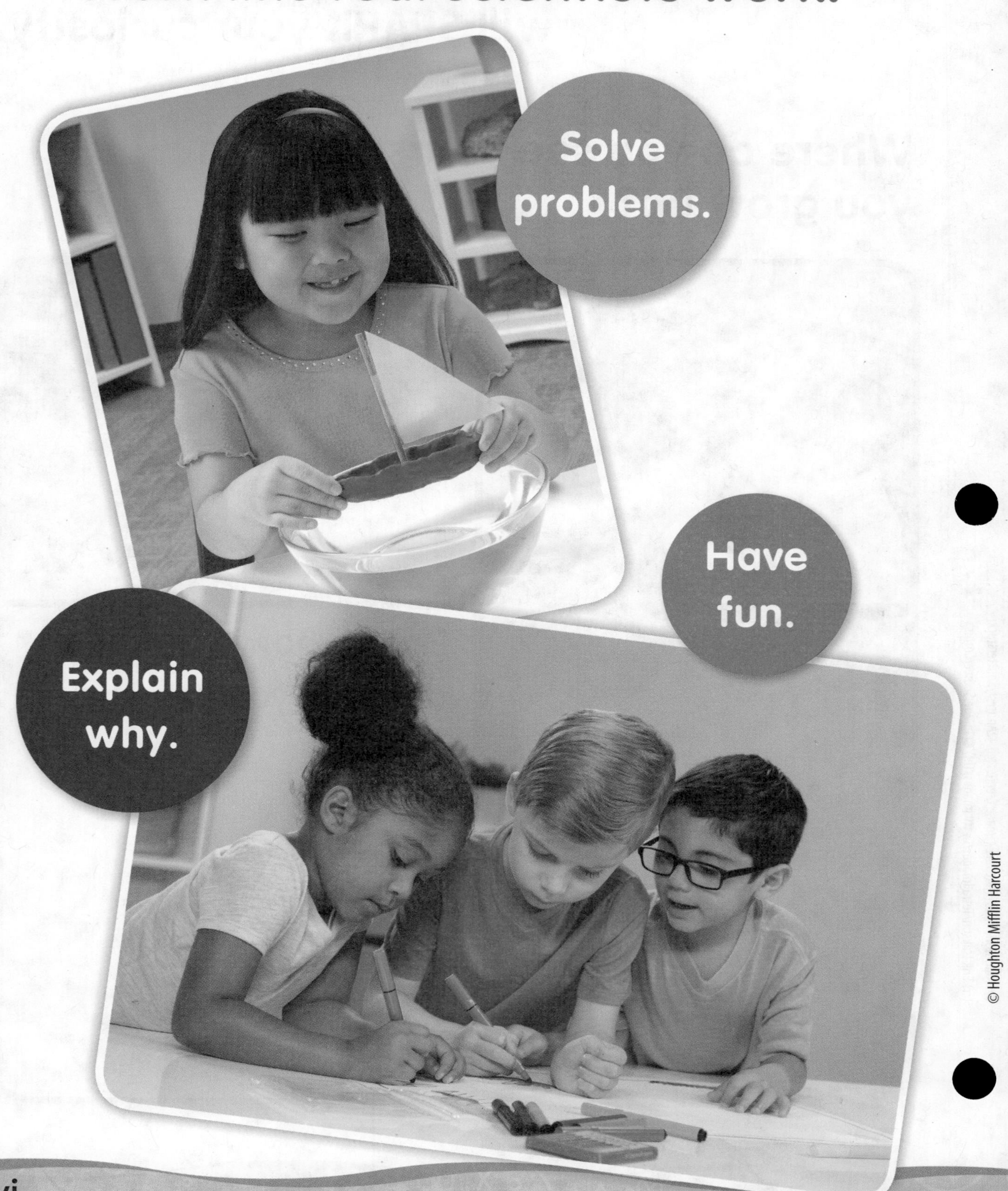

Be an engineer.
Solve problems like engineers do.

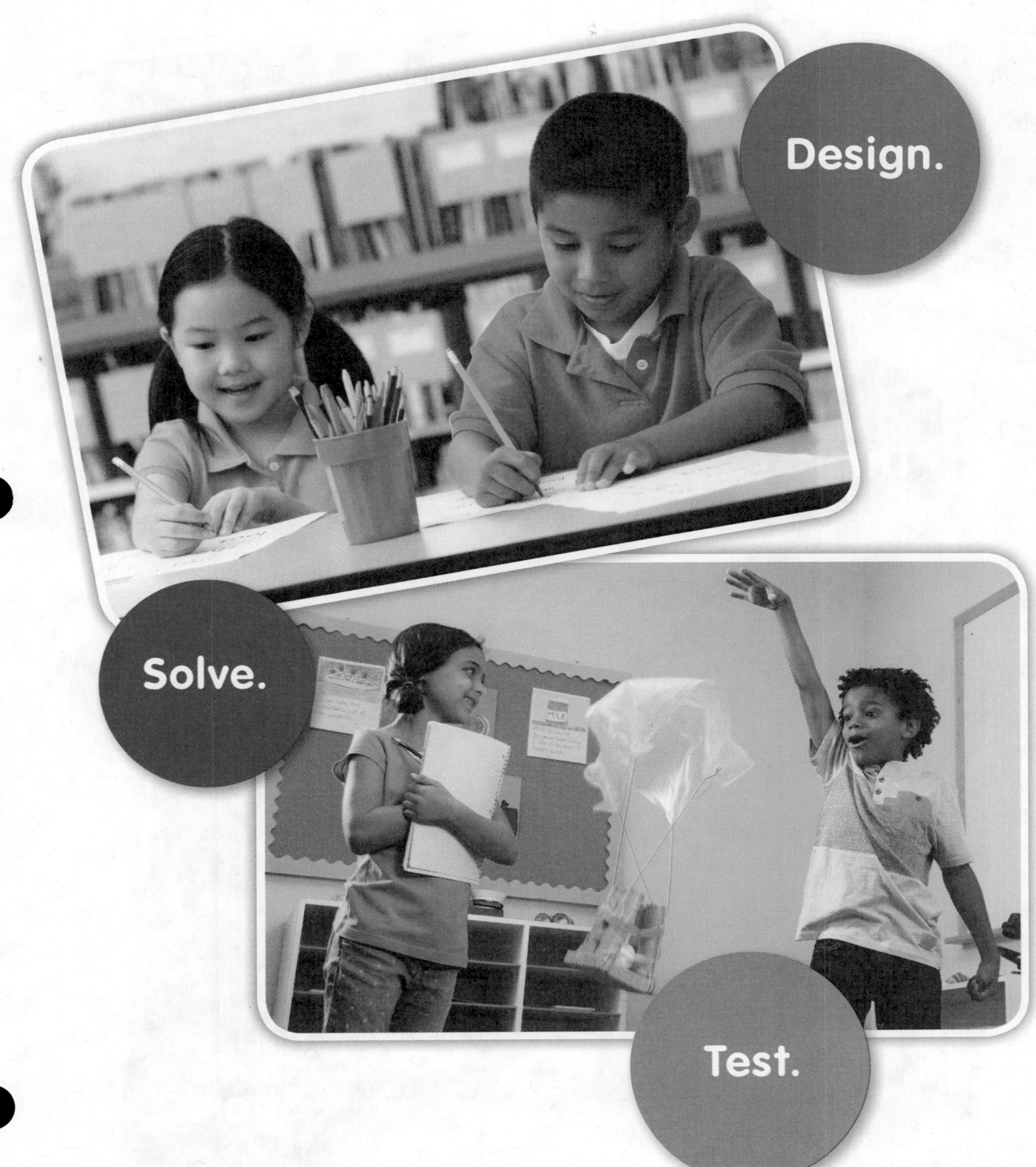

Explain your world.
Start by asking questions.

There is more than one way to the answer. What is yours?

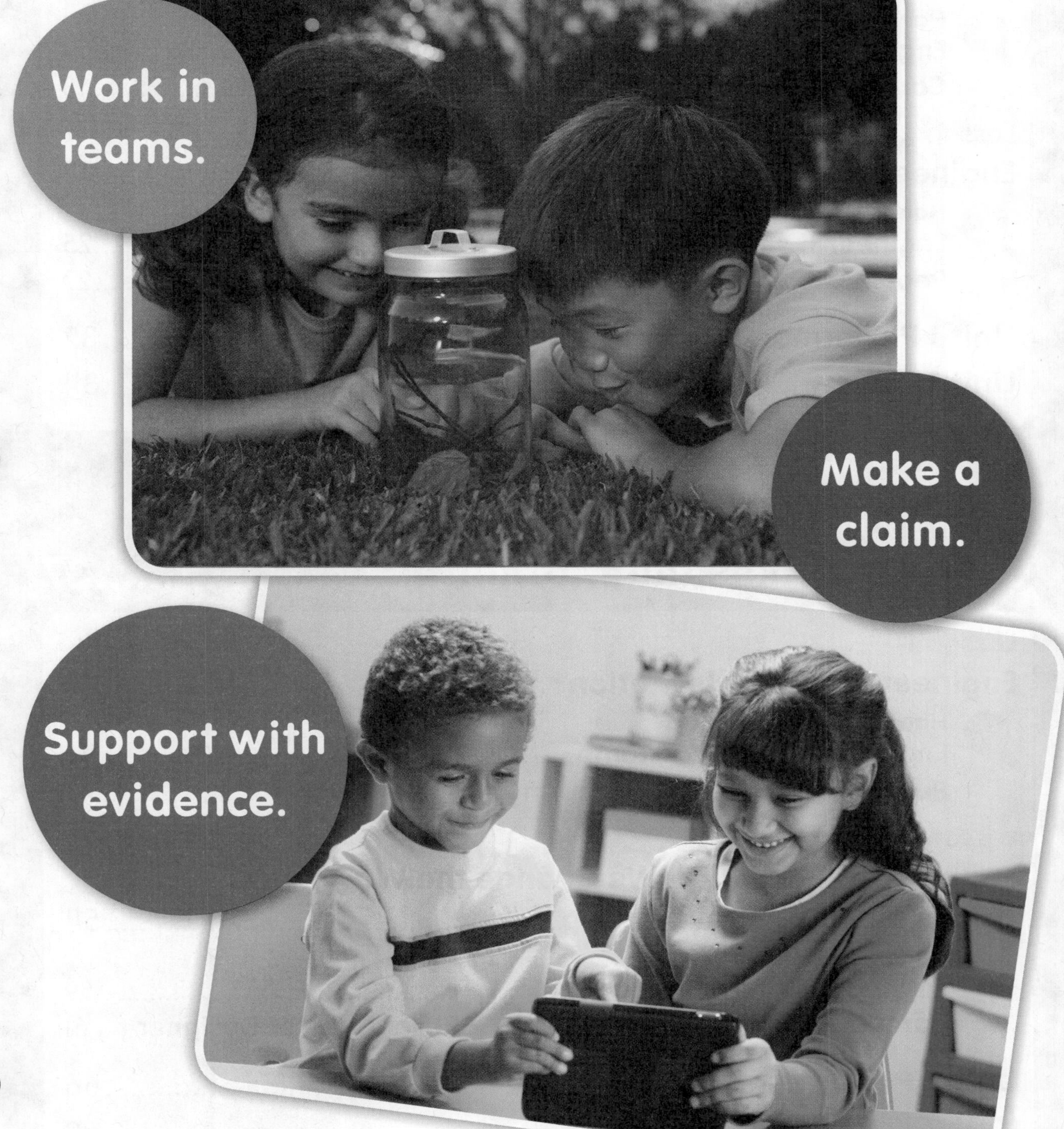

Life Science

Unit 3 • Plants and Animals 71

Earth and Space Sciences

Unit 5 • Weather 175

Unit 6 • Earth's Resources 243

Safety in Science

Doing science is fun. But a science lab can be dangerous. Know the safety rules and listen to your teacher.

⊘ **Do not eat or drink anything.**

⊘ **Do not touch sharp things.**

- ✔ **Wash your hands**
- ✔ **Wear goggles.**
- ✔ **Be neat and clean up spills.**
- ✔ **Tell your teacher if something breaks.**
- ✔ **Show good behavior.**

Are safety rules being followed?

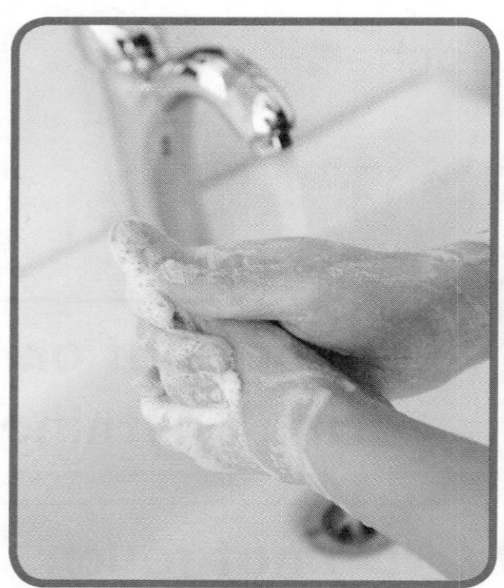

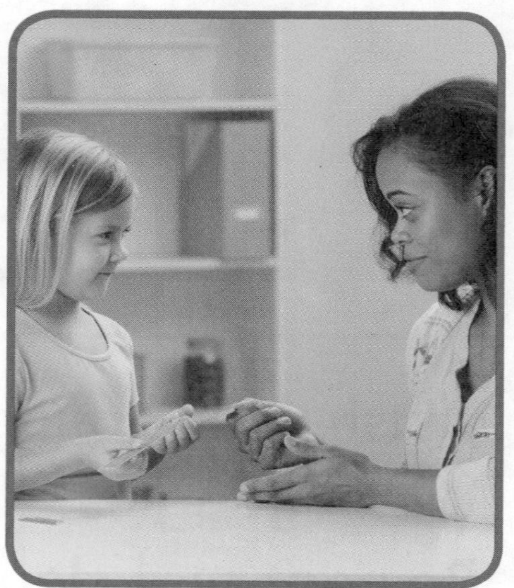

Circle the pictures where a safety rule is being followed.
Place an X on the pictures where a safety rule is not being followed.

Unit 1
Engineering and Technology

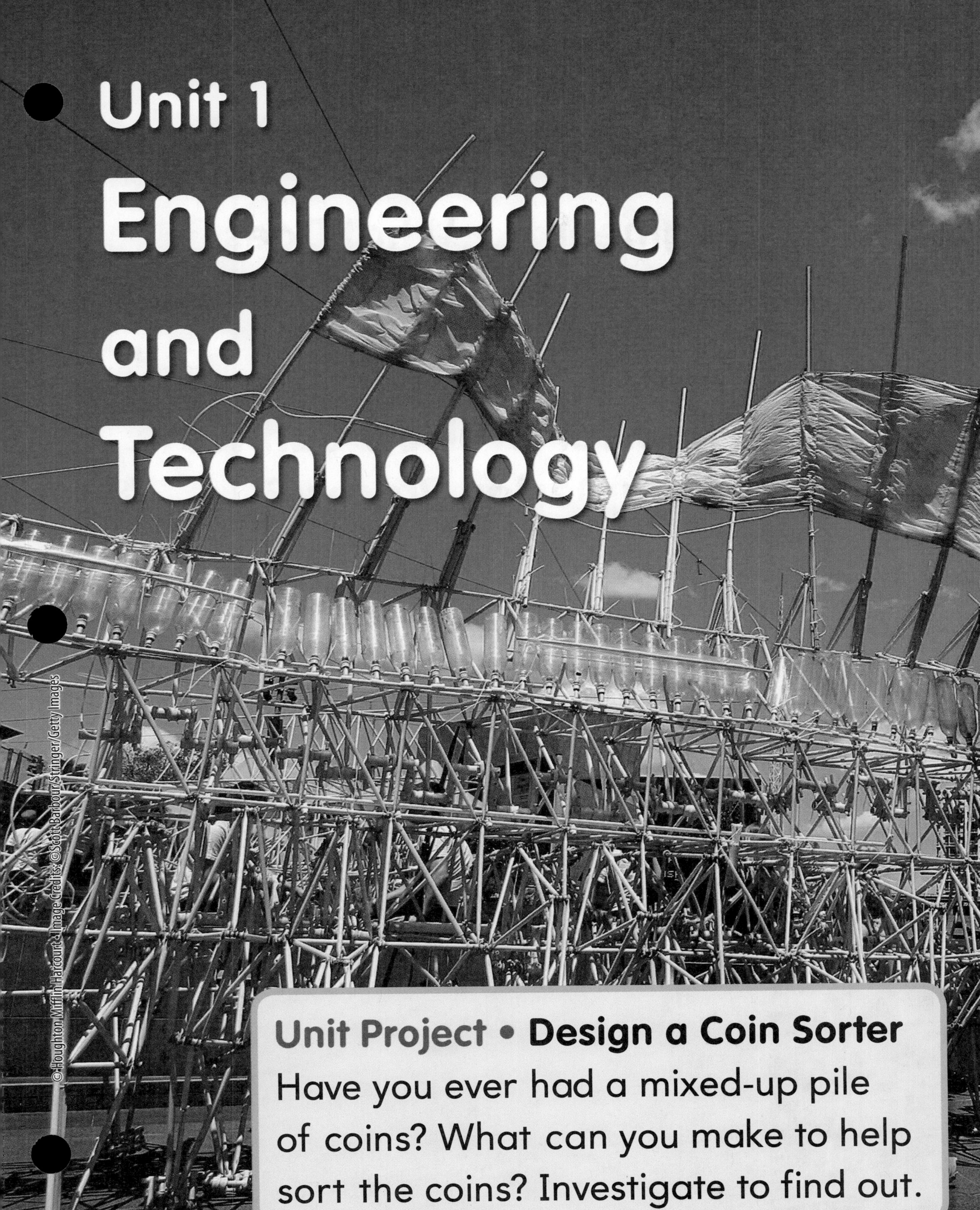

Unit Project • Design a Coin Sorter

Have you ever had a mixed-up pile of coins? What can you make to help sort the coins? Investigate to find out.

Unit 1 At a Glance

Unit Vocabulary

problem something that needs to be fixed or made better (p. 6)

solution something that fixes a problem (p. 7)

engineer someone who uses math and science to solve problems (p. 11)

technology used to solve problems (p. 12)

design process steps that solve problems (p. 20)

model something that shows what an object looks like and how it works (p. 20)

Vocabulary Game • Draw the Word!

Materials

- one set of word cards

How to Play

1. Make cards.
2. Place the cards in a pile.
3. One player picks a card and draws a picture.
4. The other player guesses the word.

Lesson 1 Engineer It • What Does an Engineer Do?

By the End of This Lesson
I will be able to tell how an engineer defines problems and comes up with solutions.

Solve a Problem

The flying disc is stuck in the tree. How can they get it down?

Can You Solve It?

Circle the pictures that show solutions to the problem.

Problems and Solutions

Explore online.

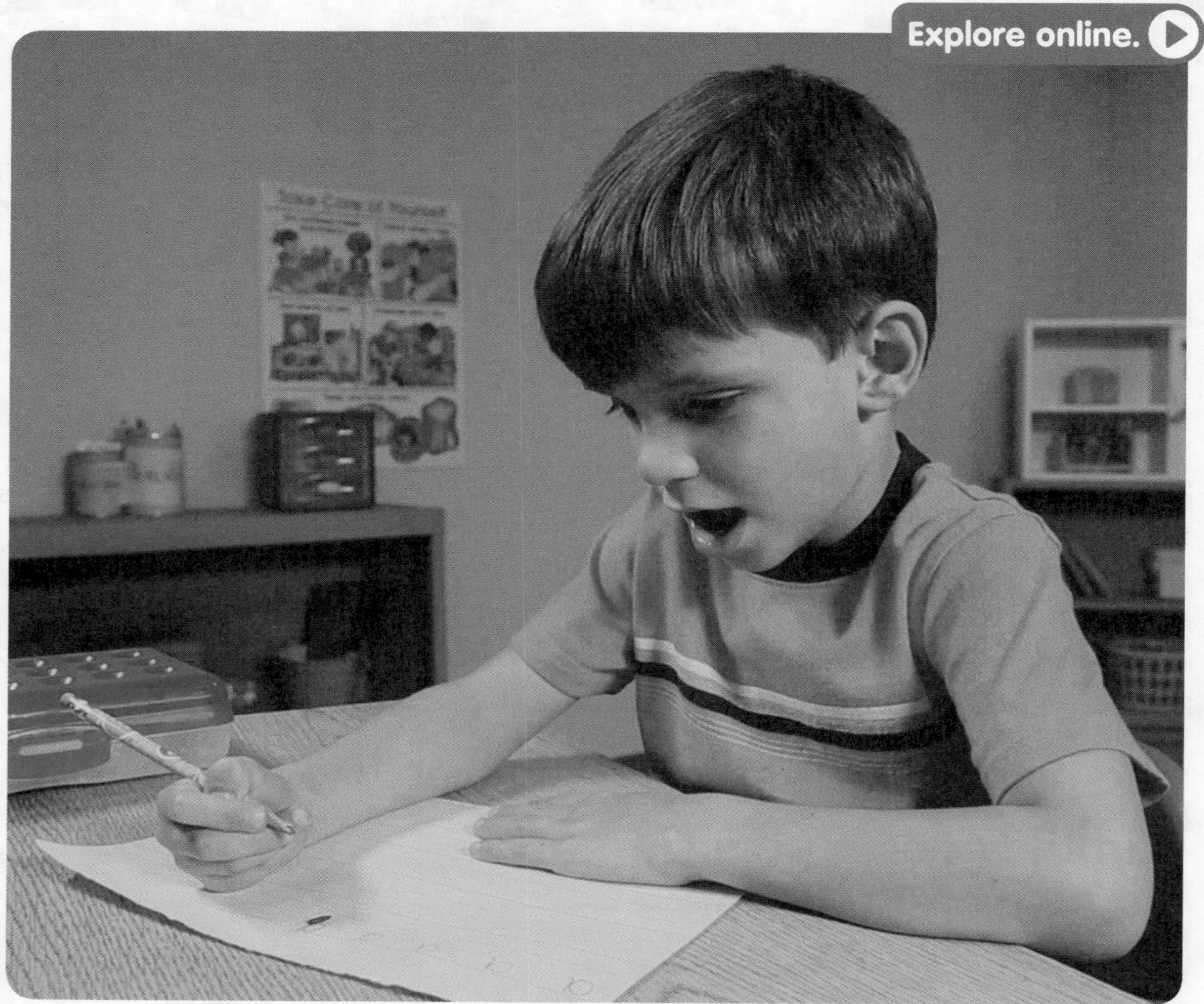

A **problem** is something that needs to be fixed or made better. You can observe to help solve a problem.

Discuss the problem that needs to be fixed.

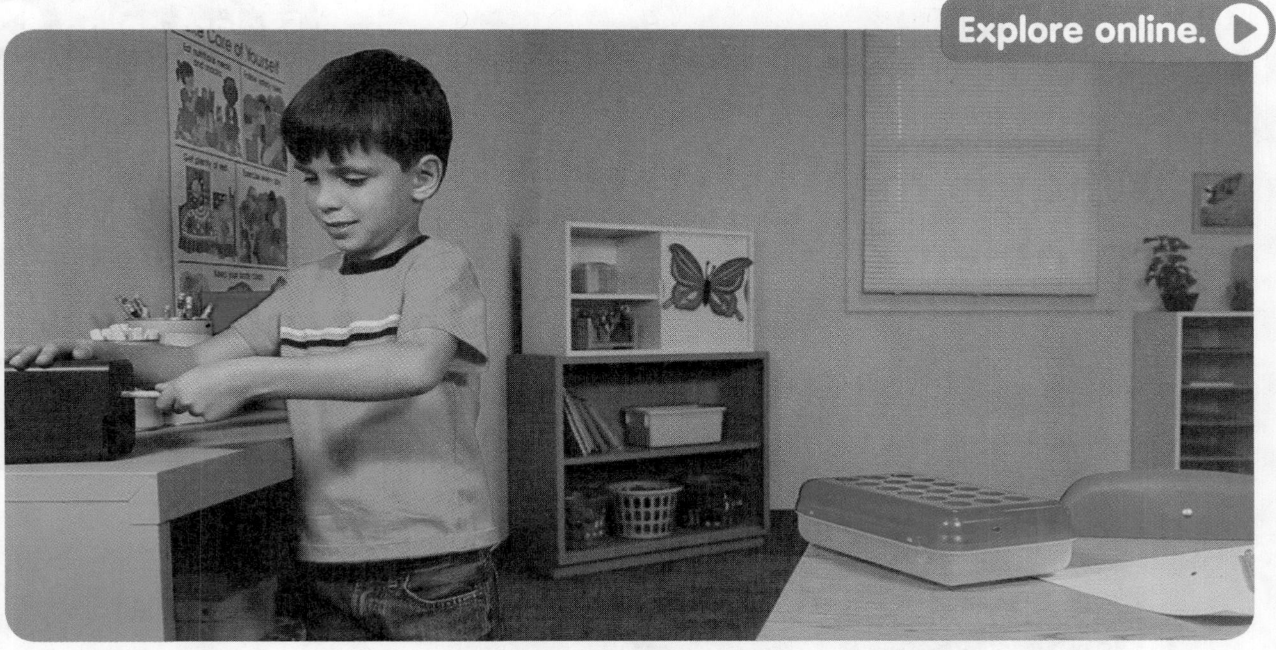

A problem may have many solutions. A **solution** is something that helps fix a problem.

Draw a picture that shows another solution to the problem. Share your idea.

Explore online.

What is the problem?

How will my idea help solve the problem?

Why is this a good solution?

Asking questions is part of solving problems.

Apply What You Know Read, Write, Share!

Ask and Answer Questions Go to the online handbook for tips.

• Circle the question words **"what," "how,"** and **"why."** ▲ Work with a partner to define a problem. Ask questions about the problem. Share your ideas with the class.

Name ______________________________

Hands-On Activity

Engineer It • Problem and Solution

Explore online.

Materials

How do you define a problem and design a solution?

Step 1

Observe the box and the objects in it.

Step 2

Define a problem with the box of supplies.

Step 3

Ask a question about the problem.

Step 4

Design a solution to solve the problem.

Draw a picture of your design.

Make a claim.

What is your evidence?

Engineers

An **engineer** uses math and science to help solve problems.

• Circle the engineer fixing a robot. ▲ Circle the things an engineer can design and build.

Technology is what engineers make and use to solve problems. Both a desk and a phone are kinds of technology.

▲

Asking Questions and Defining Problems Go to the online handbook for tips.

● Circle the examples of technology. ▲ Draw a picture of how technology has helped you solve a problem. Share your picture. Use evidence to explain how technology helped you solve the problem.

Take It Further

Explore more online.

Changes in Technology

Careers in Science & Engineering •

Toy Engineer

Explore online.

Toy engineers draw a toy. Then they make the toy and test it. They may change the toy before it is finished.

Do the Math!

Toy engineers designed this puzzle. What shapes did they use?

Count and Compare Go to the online handbook for tips.

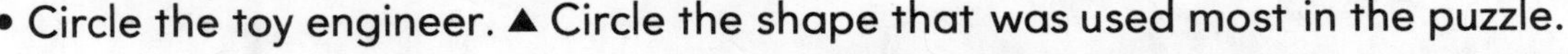

• Circle the toy engineer. ▲ Circle the shape that was used most in the puzzle.

Design a Toy

Draw

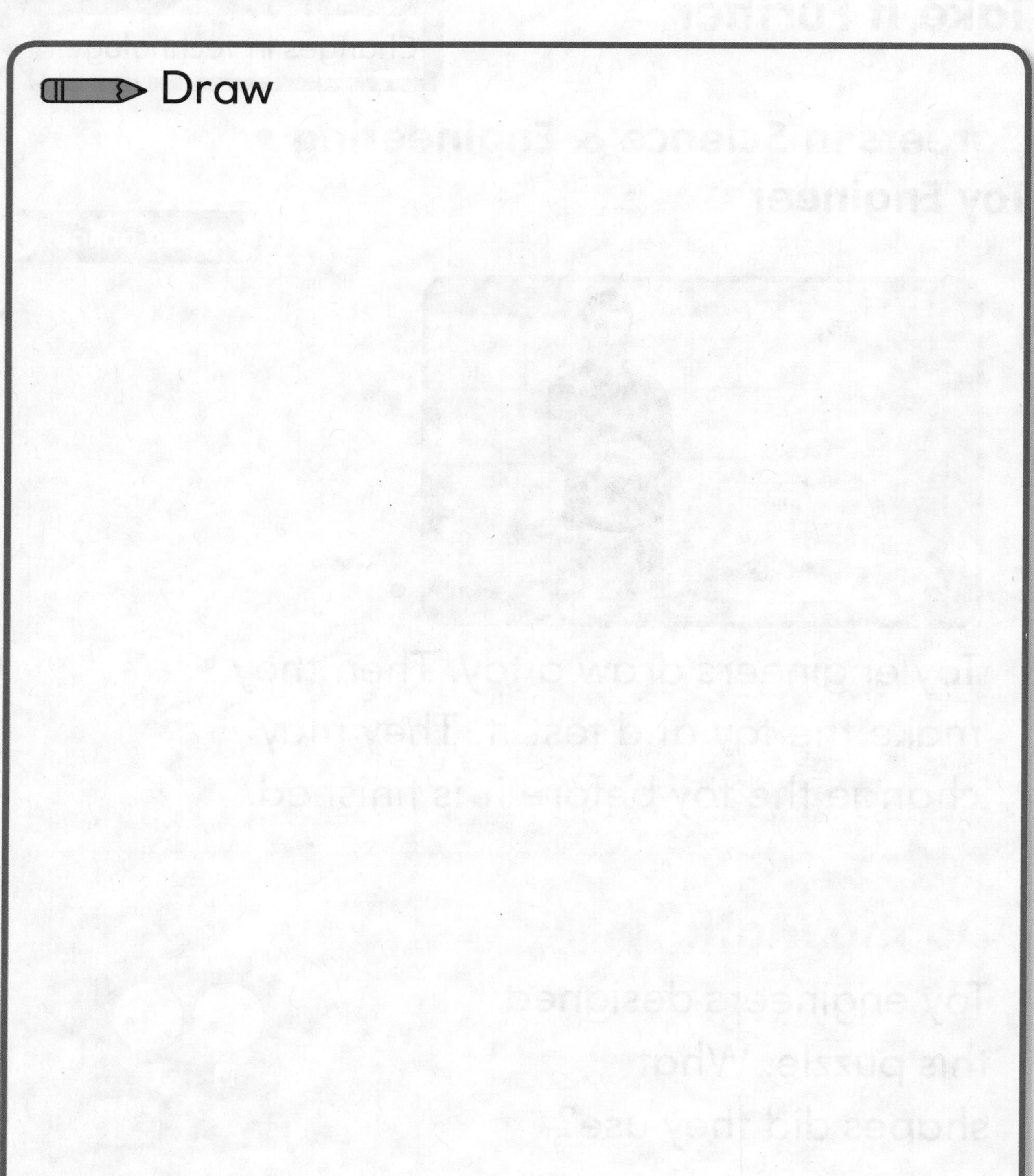

Draw your favorite toy. Write a question you have for a toy engineer.

Name ______________________

Lesson Check

The flying disc is stuck in the tree.
How can they get it down?

Circle the pictures that show solutions to the problem.

Self Check

1

- ● Circle the picture that shows a problem that can be solved.
- ▲ The toy will not fit in the gift box. Circle the pictures that show ways to solve the problem.

3

4

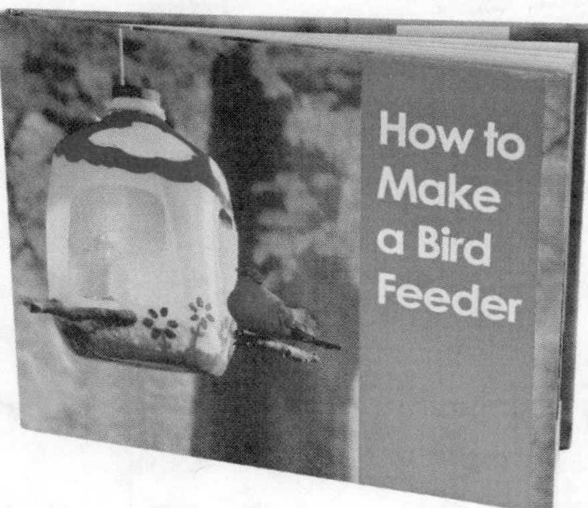

■ Circle the place where water could have gotten into the playhouse.

✱ Circle the pictures that show something that could help you build a bird feeder.

Lesson 2 Engineer It • How Can We Use a Design Process?

By the End of This Lesson

I will be able to use a design process to define and solve a problem.

Light Problem

A ballpark is a place where people play baseball.

Explore online.

Can You Solve It?

Where would you put lights so people can see when it is dark? Draw an X on the places where you think lights should go.

A Design Process

A **design process** is a set of five steps that engineers follow to solve problems.

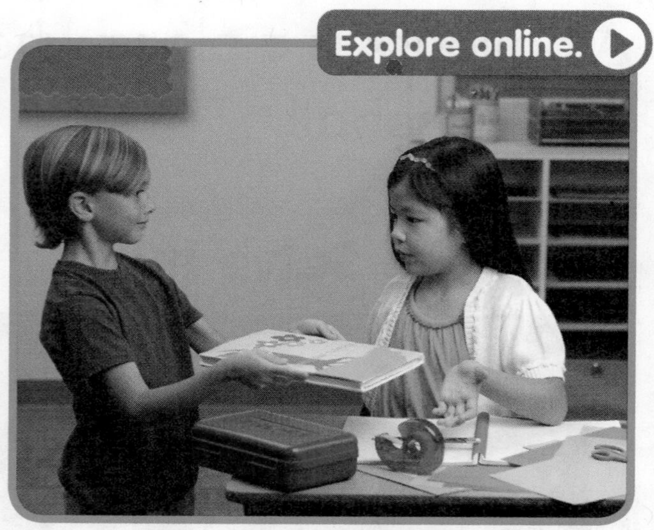

Step 1 Define a Problem

Define a problem that needs solving.

Asking Questions and Defining Problems Go to the online handbook for tips.

Step 2 Plan and Build

Plan your design.
Then build a model.
A **model** of something shows what it looks like and how it works.

Defining and Delimiting Engineering Problems Go to the online handbook for tips.

Circle the children building models of their design.

Do the Math!

Look at the pictures. Circle the cylinder.

Name Shapes Go to the online handbook for tips.

Apply What You Know **Evidence Notebook**

Use Visuals Go to the online handbook for tips.

• Circle the cylinder. ▲ In your Evidence Notebook draw which tower you think will work best. Use evidence to tell why you think that.

Step 3 Test and Improve

Explore online.

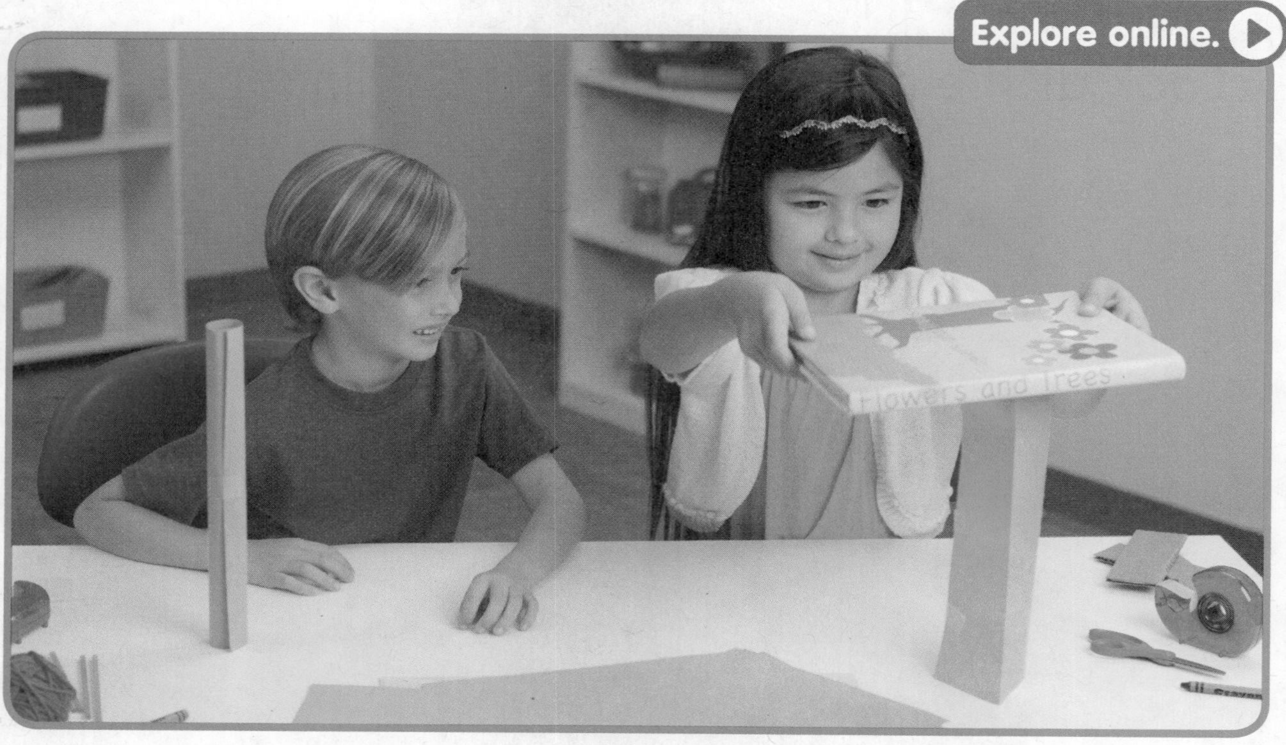

Test your solution to see if it works.
Make it better if you can.

Draw two different ways you could make the towers better.

Step 4 Redesign

Explore online.

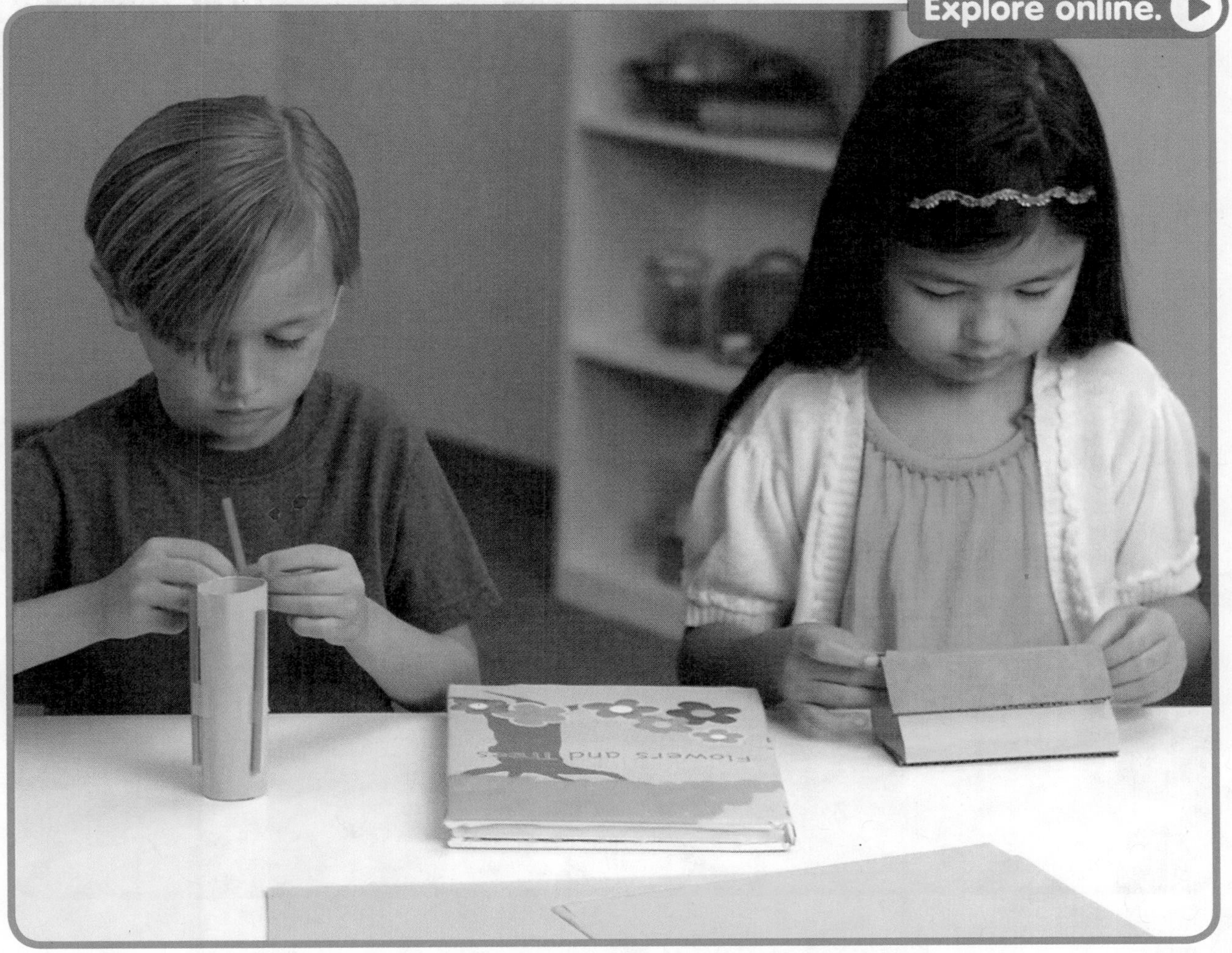

When you redesign something, you design it again to make it better.

Apply What You Know Evidence Notebook

Think about a problem that needs a solution. Write or draw about the problem. Use evidence to tell how a design process would help you find a solution.

Step 5 Communicate

Explore online.

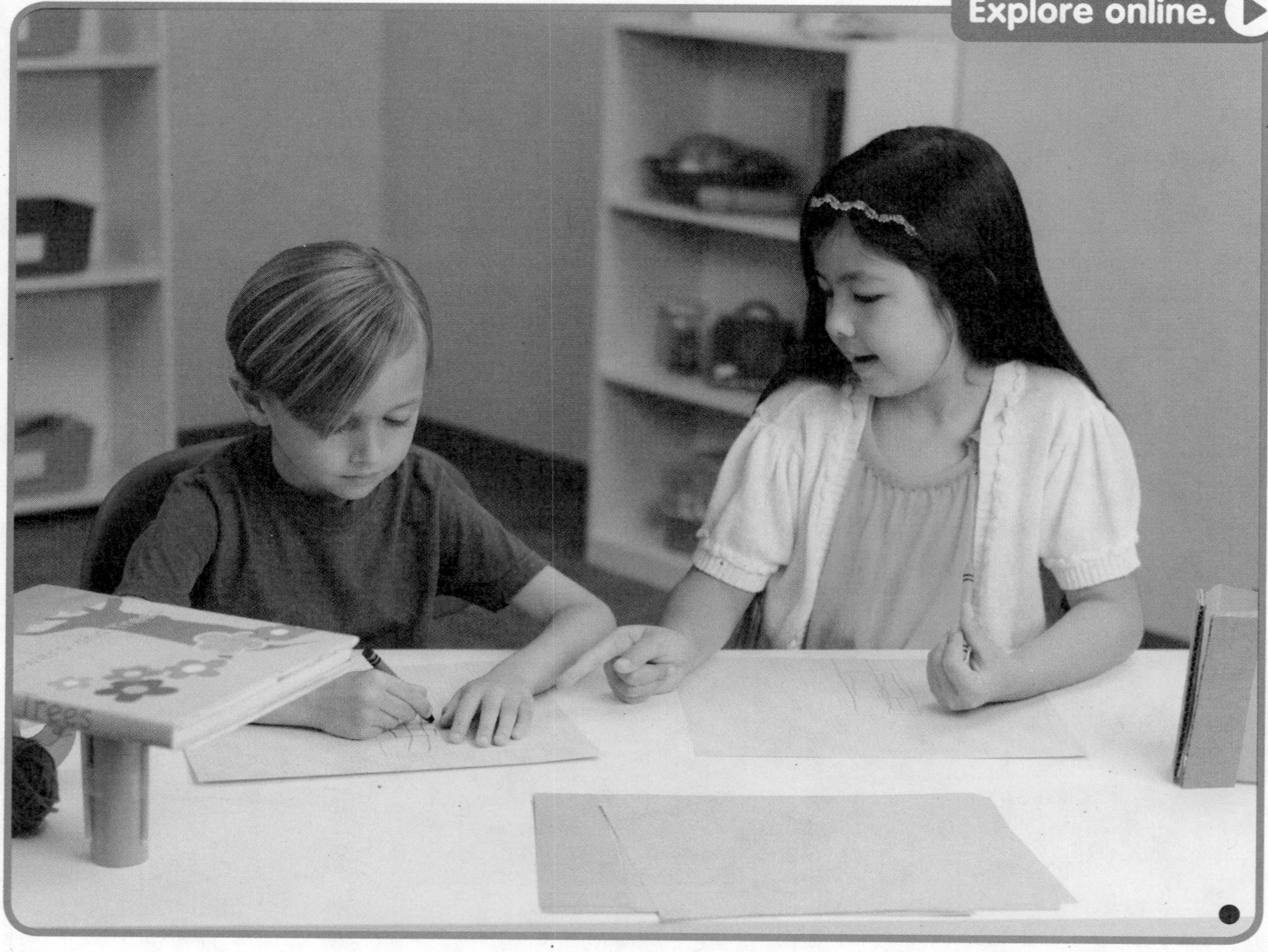

When you communicate, you share what you learned with others.

Use Visuals Go to the online handbook for tips. 

• Draw a line under what the children are using to communicate a solution. ▲ Pick one step in the design process. Draw a picture or tell about a time you used it.

Name ______________________

Hands-On Activity

Engineer It • A Design Process

Explore online.

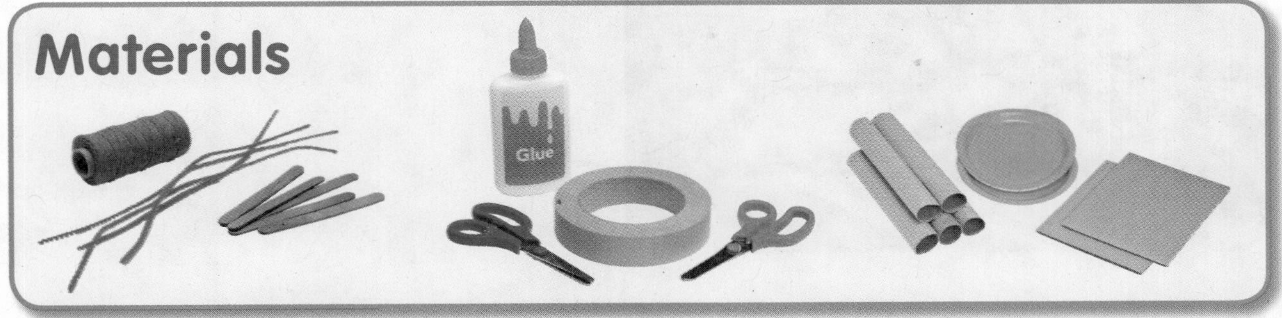

How can you make a tool to reach something under a couch?

Step 1

Define the problem.

Step 2

Plan two ways to solve the problem. Build your tools.

Step 3

Test your tools.

Step 4

Redesign the tools to make them better.
Retest your tools.

Step 5

Share your tools. Compare designs.

Make a claim.

What is your evidence?

Take It Further

Explore more online.

Paper Tower Project

People in Science & Engineering • Dr. Ayanna Howard

Dr. Ayanna Howard is a robot engineer. She designs and makes robots. She uses people as models for making them.

Circle the picture of Dr. Howard holding one of her robots.

Robot

Draw a picture of a robot that can tie a shoe.

Name ______________________

Lesson Check

A ballpark is a place where people play baseball.

Explore online.

Can You Solve It?

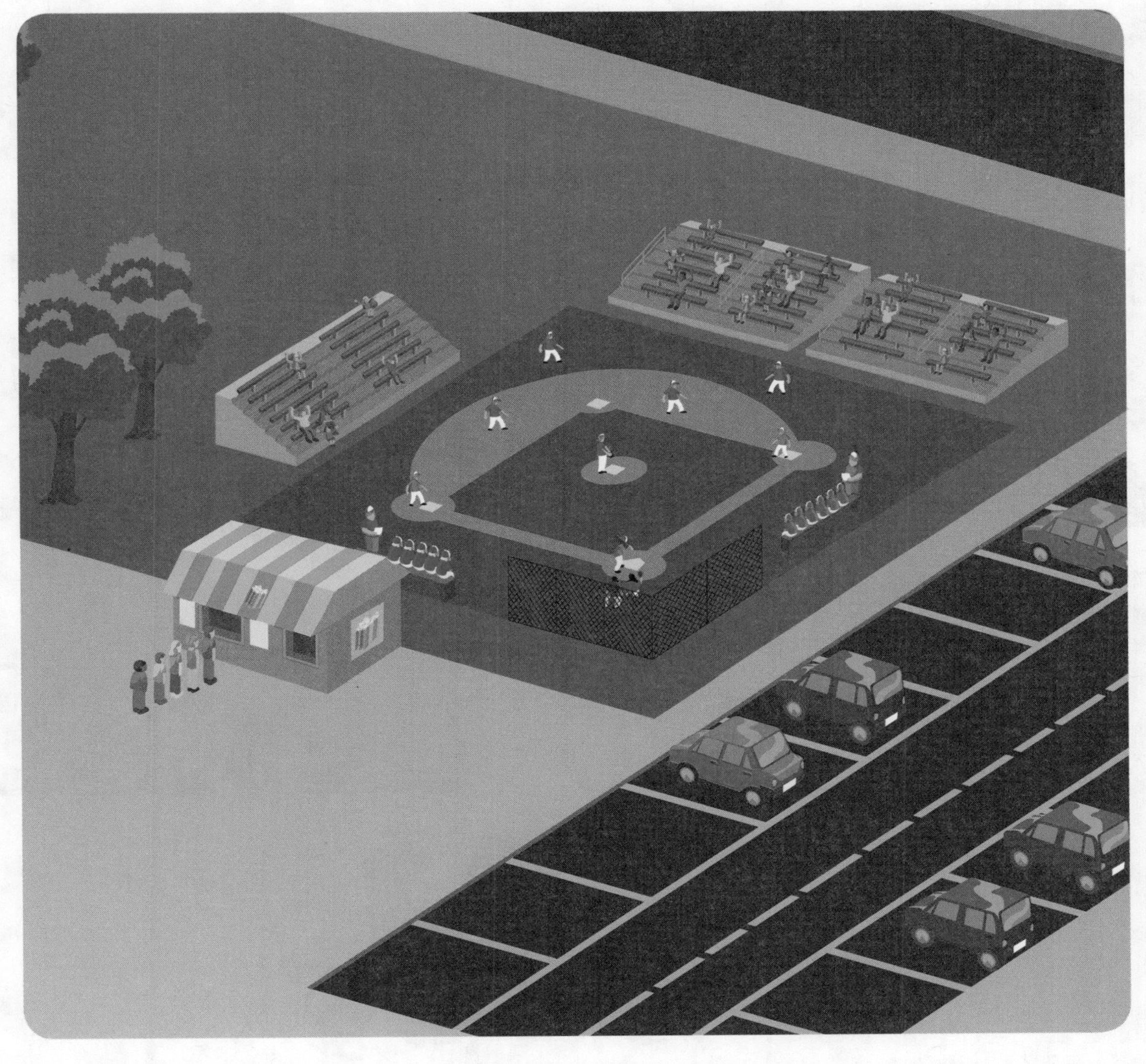

Where would you put lights so people can see when it is dark? Draw an X on the places where you think lights should go.

Self Check

1

● Number the pictures from 1 to 3 to show the steps in the design process.

▲ Circle the child communicating a solution to the problem.

3

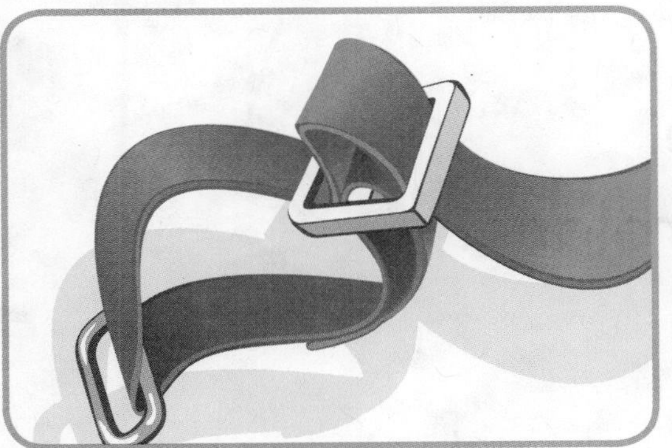

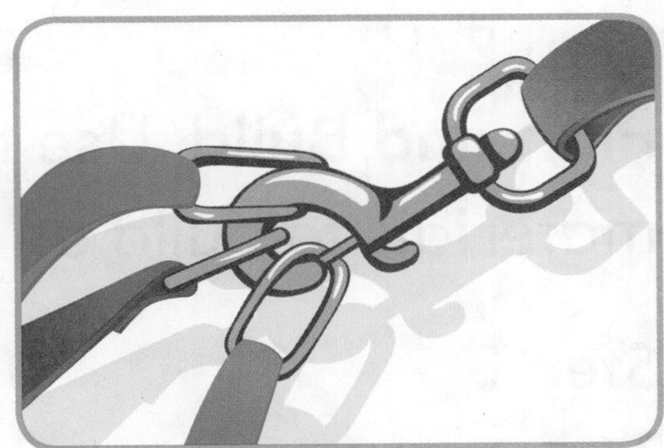

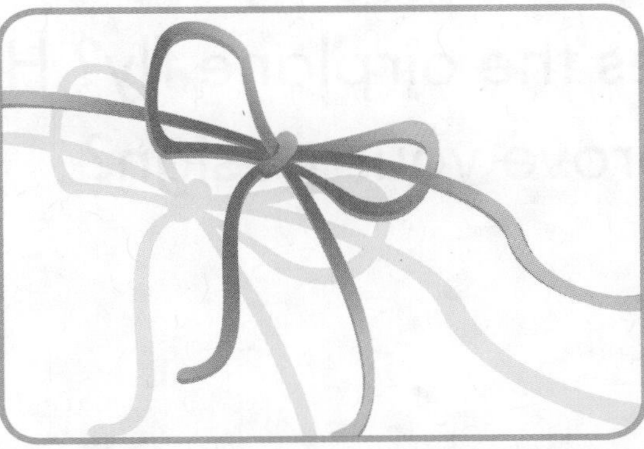

■ Circle the picture that shows what the child does after testing a solution.

✱ Circle the picture that shows the best solution for holding the leashes together.

Unit 1 Performance Task

Engineer It • Build an Airplane

Materials

- a straw that does not bend
- construction paper
- safety scissors
- tape

STEPS

Step 1

Define a Problem Build an airplane and see how far it can fly.

Step 2

Plan and Build Use the materials to build an airplane.

Step 3

Test and Improve Test your design. How far does the airplane fly? How can you improve your design?

Step 4

Redesign Build a better airplane by making changes to the materials or the way they are used.

Step 5

Communicate Show how far your airplane can fly. Explain how you improved your design.

Check

_____ I built an airplane that flies.

_____ I tested my airplane.

_____ I redesigned my airplane so it flies farther.

_____ I shared my design with others.

Unit 1 Review

Name ______________________________

1

- ● Draw a line to match the problem and the solution.
- ▲ Which pictures show a possible solution to the problem? Circle the correct pictures.

3

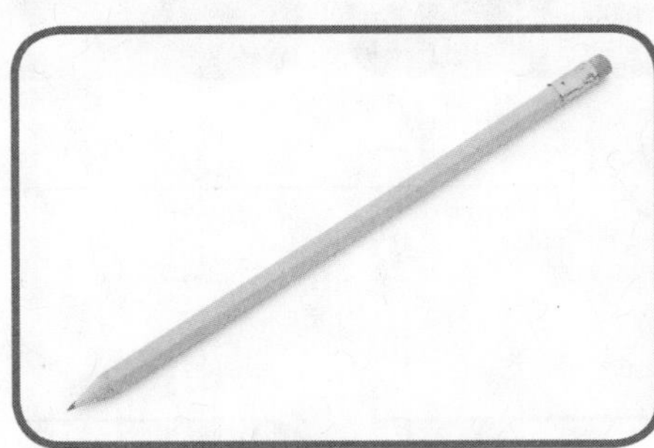

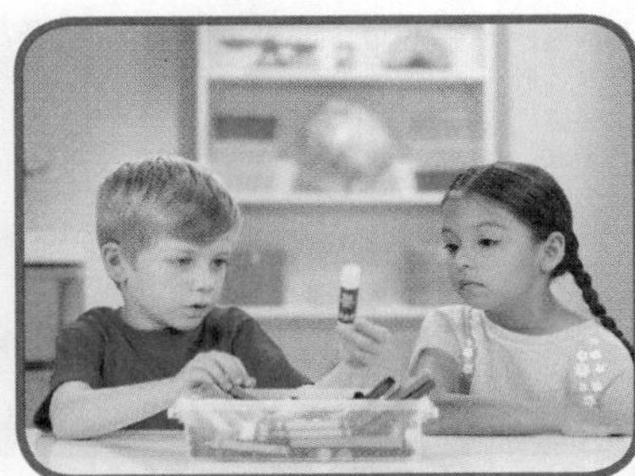

■ Which picture shows an engineer planning a design? Circle the correct picture.
✱ Which pictures show technology? Circle the correct pictures.
● Which picture shows the children redesigning their tool? Circle the correct picture.

7

8

▲ Which picture shows an engineer building a model? Circle the correct picture.

■ Which picture shows a girl testing her design for a toy? Circle the correct picture.

✷ Which picture shows how the girl is communicating about the toy she made? Circle the correct picture.

Unit 2
Forces and Motion

Unit Project • A Game of Motion

How can you score points with a little push? Investigate to find out.

Unit 2 At a Glance

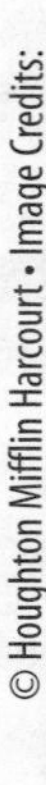

Unit Vocabulary

motion the act of moving (p. 42)

speed how fast or slow something moves (p. 44)

direction the path a moving object takes (p. 47)

force a push or a pull that can make an object at rest move or an object in motion stop (p. 56)

Vocabulary Game • Guess the Word!

Materials

- one set of word cards

How to Play

1. Make cards. Place them in a pile.
2. One player picks a card.
3. That player acts out the word.
4. The other player guesses the word.

Lesson 1 Engineer It • What Is Motion?

By the End of This Lesson

I will be able to tell about the motion, speed, and direction of objects.

Pushes and Pulls

Explore online.

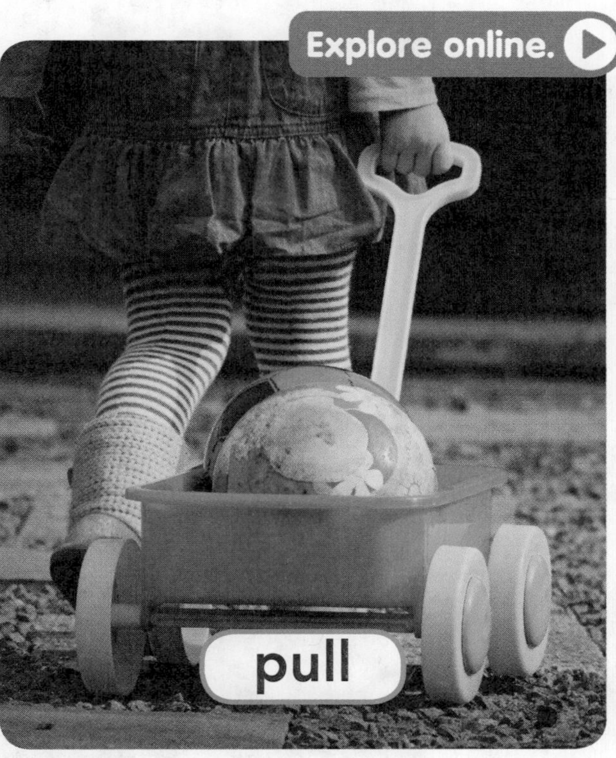

Can You Explain It?

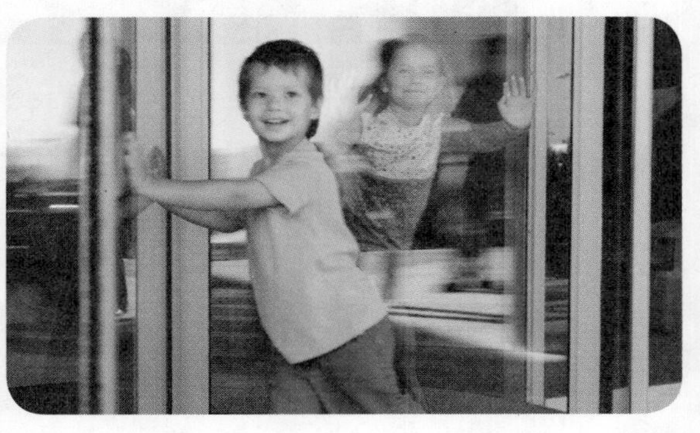

▲

• Think about pushes and pulls. How do they move things differently? ▲ Circle the picture that shows a push. Draw a line under the picture that shows a pull.

Motion

Explore online.

pull

push

Motion is the act of moving. When something is moving, it is in motion.

Scientific Investigations Use a Variety of Methods Go to the online handbook for tips.

Circle the things that are in motion.

A push or a pull can make something move. They can also stop something from moving.

Apply What You Know **Evidence Notebook**

Scientific Investigations Use a Variety of Methods Go to the online handbook for tips.

• Circle all the pictures that show something being pushed. ▲ Find something that is moving. Use evidence to explain how you know it is moving.

Speed

Explore online. 

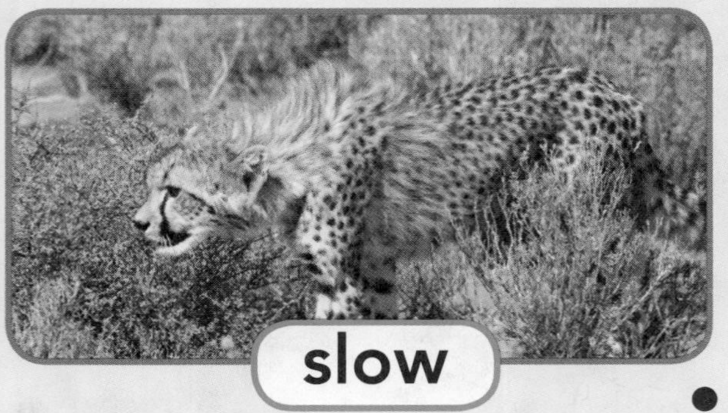

●

Some things move fast. Some things move slowly. **Speed** is how fast or slow something moves.

Scientific Investigations Use a Variety of Methods Go to the online handbook for tips. 

▲

■

● Circle the cheetah that is moving slowly. ▲ Circle the things that are moving fast. ■ Fold a sheet of paper. Write the word "fast" on one side. Draw something that moves fast. Write the word "slow" on the other side. Draw something that moves slowly. Share your drawings.

Name ____________________

Hands-On Activity

Engineer It • Make a Ramp

Explore online.

Materials

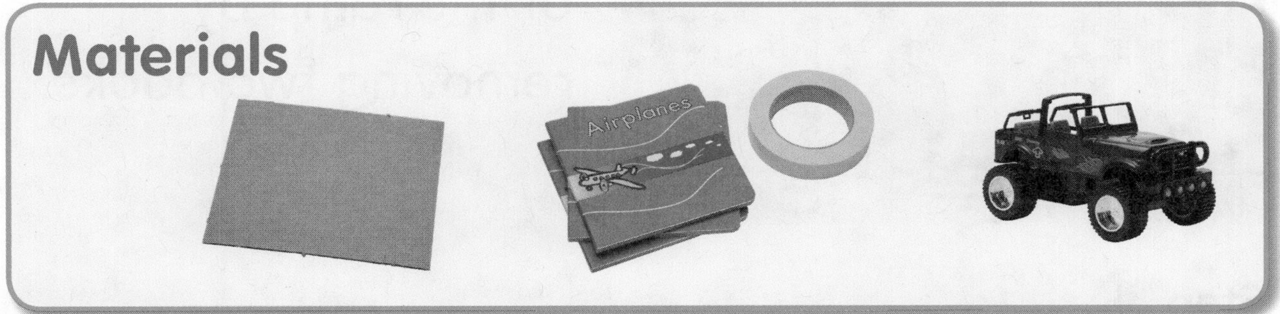

Which ramp makes the toy car go faster?

Step 1

Make a ramp. Tape the ramp to the table.

Step 2

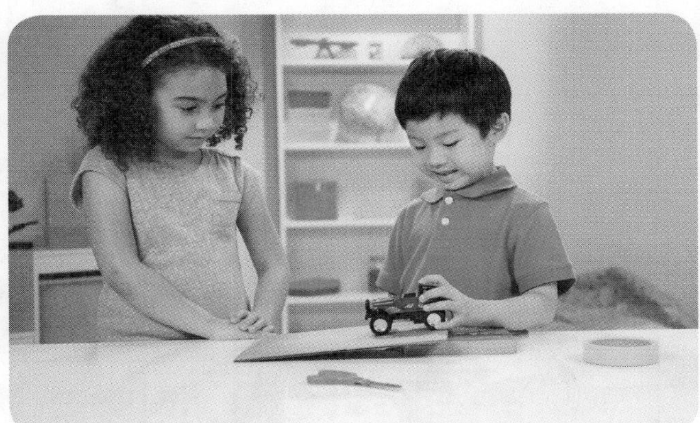

Let the car go so it rolls down the ramp.

Step 3

Change the height of the ramp by removing two books.

Step 4

Repeat the test.

Step 5

Draw conclusions. Did the height of the ramp change the speed of the car?

Make a claim.	What is your evidence?

Direction

Explore online.

up and down

zigzag

round and round

straight

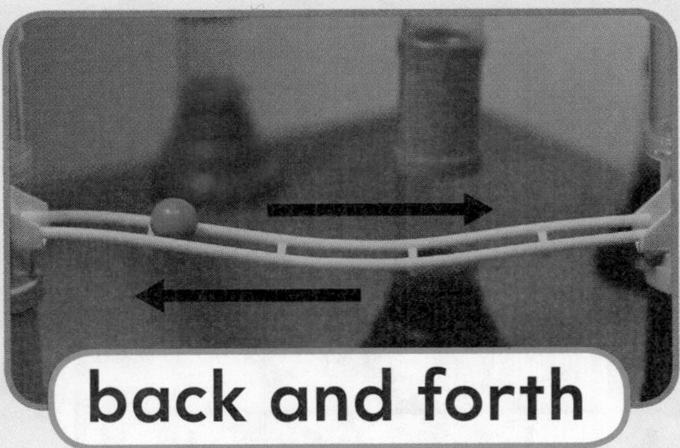

back and forth

Direction is the path a moving object takes.

Scientific Investigations Use a Variety of Methods Go to the online handbook for tips.

Look at the picture of the whole track. Color the zigzag path.

Look closely at each picture.
What direction does it show?

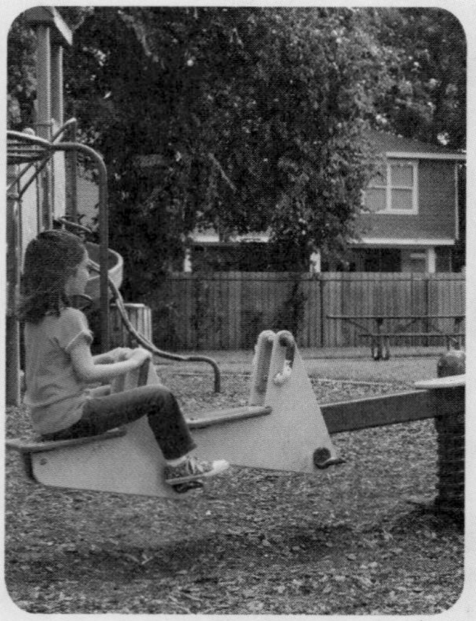

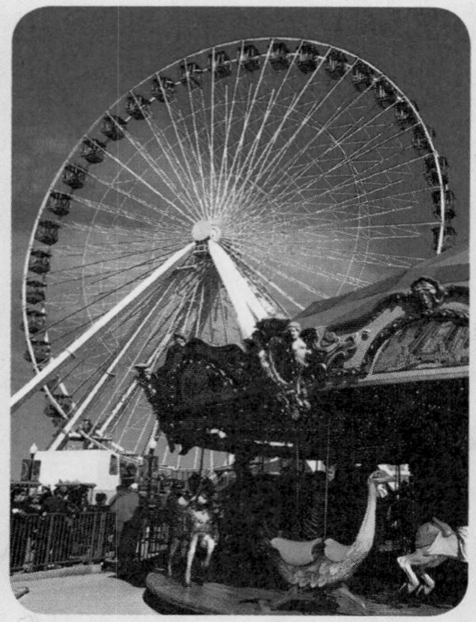

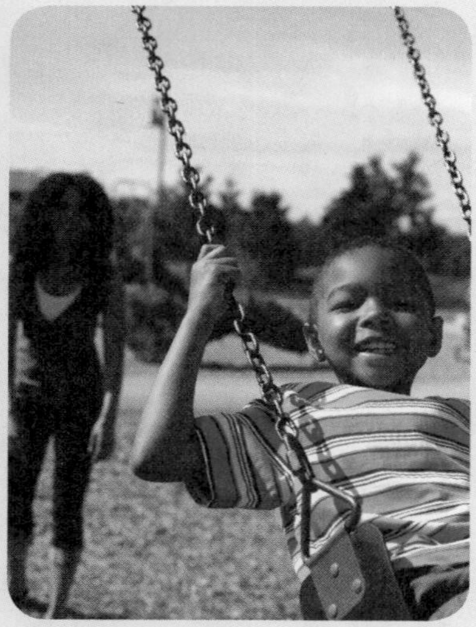

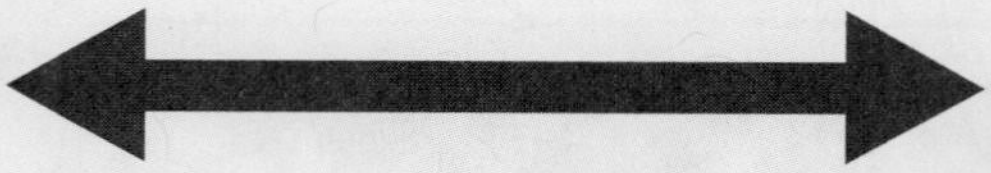

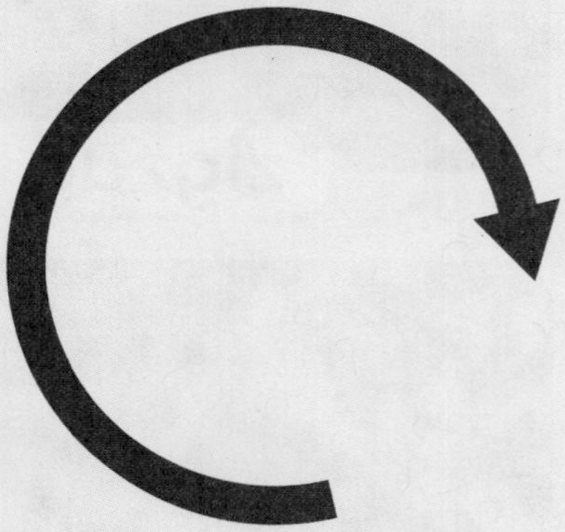

back and forth

up and down

round and round

Apply What You Know

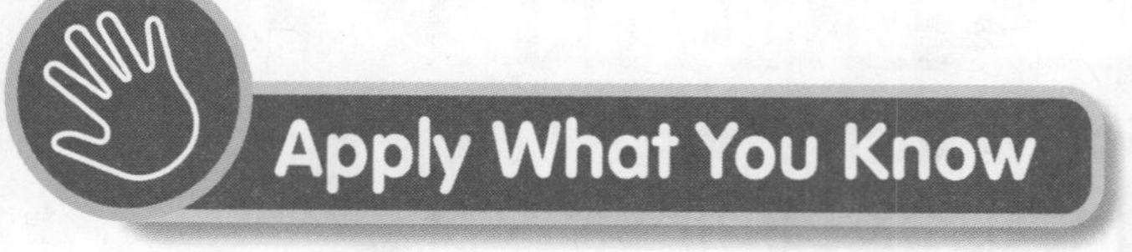

• Draw a line from each picture to an arrow that shows the direction. ▲ Play "Follow the Leader." The leader will take the group in different directions.

Take It Further

Explore more online.

Friction

People in Science & Engineering • Isaac Newton

Isaac Newton was a scientist who lived long ago. He studied how and why things move.

Read, Write, Share!

▲

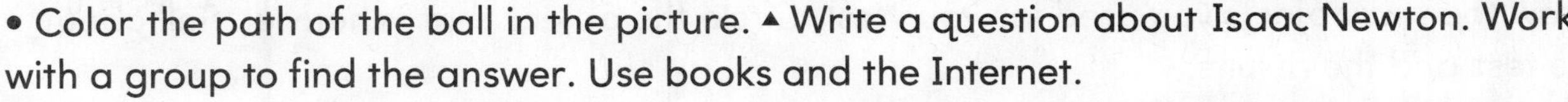

Research Project Go to the online handbook for tips.

• Color the path of the ball in the picture. ▲ Write a question about Isaac Newton. Work with a group to find the answer. Use books and the Internet.

Do a Test!

Step 1
Choose one heavy object. Choose one light object.

Step 2
Blow through a straw to move the objects.

Step 3
What was the effect of using the straw?

Cause and Effect Go to the online handbook for tips.

Do the Math!

Compare Objects Go to the online handbook for tips.

Draw the two objects you used for your test. Circle the object that is heavier. Tell about the test and the results.

Name ______________________

Lesson Check

Explore online.

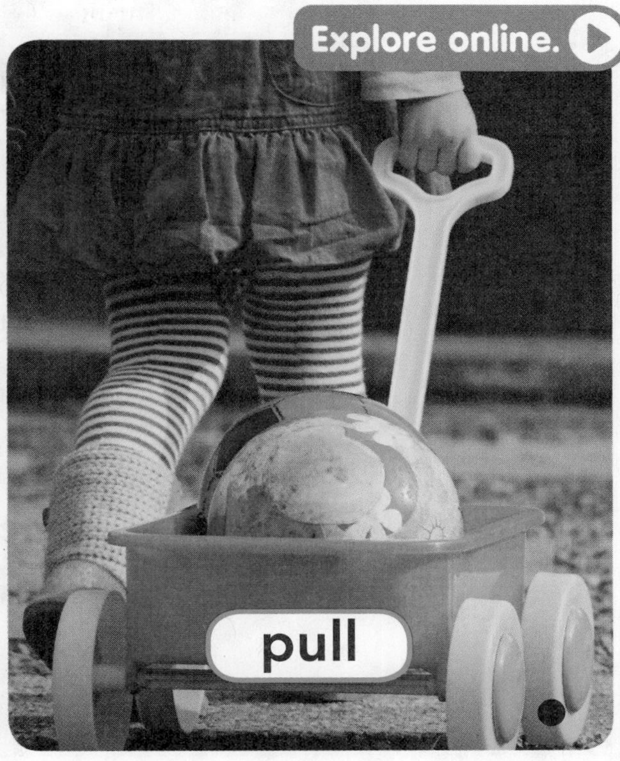

Can You Explain It?

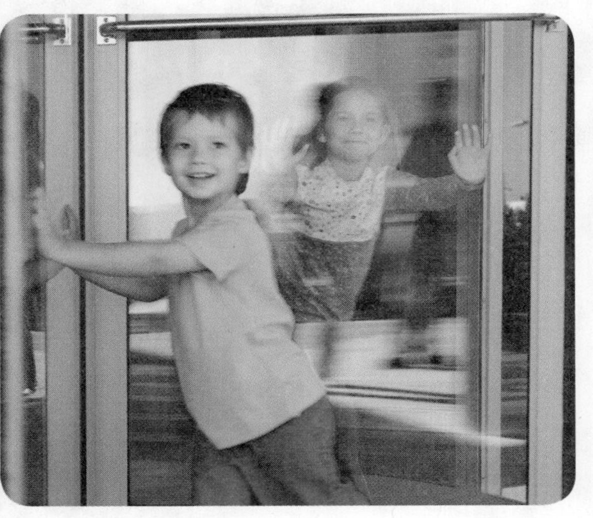

▲

• Think about pushes and pulls. How do they move things differently? ▲ Circle the picture that shows a push. Draw a line under the picture that shows a pull.

Self Check

1

● Circle the pictures that show a push. ▲ Circle the picture that shows something moving slowly.

3

4

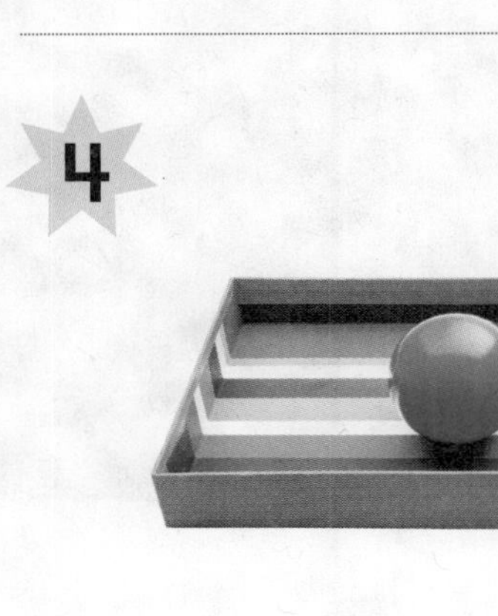

■ Circle the pictures that show a direction. ✱ Circle the picture that shows how to set up an investigation of whether a ramp changes the speed of a ball.

Lesson 2

Engineer It • How Can We Change the Way Things Move?

By the End of This Lesson

I will be able to tell how to change the speed and direction of objects.

Change Direction and Speed

What will happen to this ball?

The direction and speed of objects can change.

Can You Explain It?

• Think about how a ball moves when it has been kicked. Does it go faster or slower? In what direction does it move? ▲ Circle the pictures that show what you think the boy can do to make the ball move quickly.

Changing Speed

Explore online.

fast

slow

A **force** is a push or a pull that can make an object at rest move or an object in motion stop. Forces can also change the speed of objects.

Apply What You Know

Cause and Effect Go to the online handbook for tips.

● Circle the pictures of someone using a force to make the ball move fast. ▲ Take turns kicking a ball hard and then softly to a partner. Talk about how the different kicks affect the speed of the ball.

Changing Direction

Explore online.

Forces can change the direction objects move.

● Circle the pictures of someone using a force to change the direction the ball is moving.

▲ List more ways to change the direction of an object. Talk about cause and effect. Use evidence to support your ideas.

Bumping

Explore online.

This bowling ball caused the pins to fall down.

When objects touch, they push one another. The push can make the objects change direction and speed. ●

Apply What You Know Do the Math! ▲

Compare Objects Go to the online handbook for tips.

● Circle the objects changing direction because they are being bumped. ▲ Talk about how one marble hitting another marble affects its speed and direction.

Name ______________________

Hands-On Activity

Engineer It • Pushing Objects

Explore online.

Materials

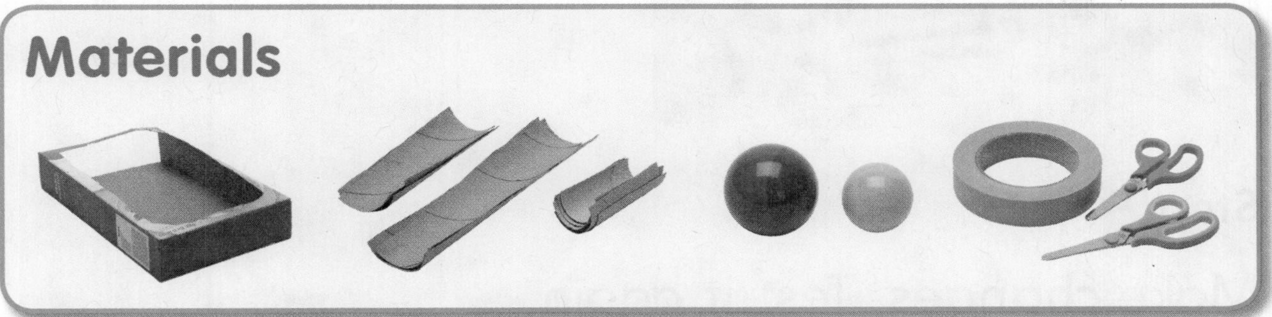

What happens when two objects push each other?

Step 1

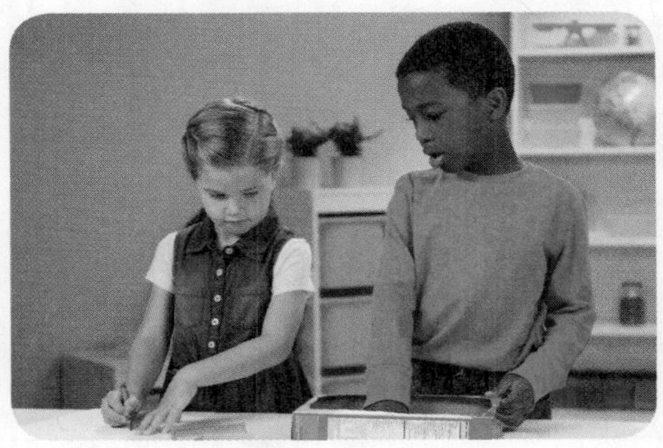

Design a marble track. The marble should change direction, change speed, and push another marble.

Step 2

Build the track.

Step 3

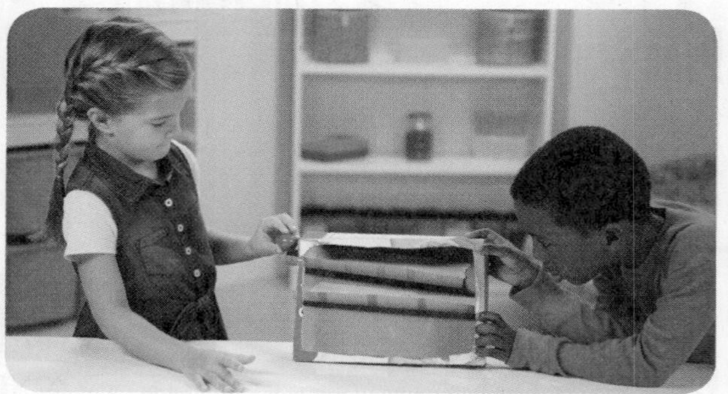

Test the track.

Observe.

Step 4

Make changes. Test it again.

Step 5

Analyze your results.

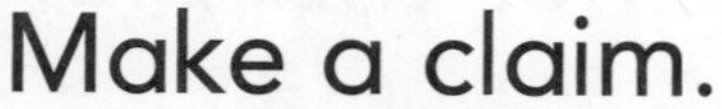

Make a claim.

What is your evidence?

Take It Further

Explore more online.

Balloon Rocket Racers

Careers in Science & Engineering • Roller Coaster Designer

Explore online.

Engineers design roller coasters. They must keep safety in mind as they plan the ride.

Circle the picture of an engineer building a roller coaster.

Design Your Own Roller Coaster

Draw

Read, Write, Share!

▲

Ask and Answer Questions Go to the online handbook for tips.

• Draw a picture of a roller coaster you design. Tell about the speed and motion of the ride. ▲ Think of questions you have about roller coasters. Find the answers in books or on the Internet. Share what you learn.

Name ____________________

Lesson Check

What will happen to this ball?

Explore online.

The direction and speed of objects can change.

Can You Explain It?

• Think about how a ball moves when it has been kicked. Does it go faster or slower? In what direction does it move? ▲ Circle the pictures that show what you think the boy can do to make the ball move quickly.

Self Check

1

● Circle the pictures of a pull being used to move something. ▲ Circle the picture of a way to make an object stop moving.

3

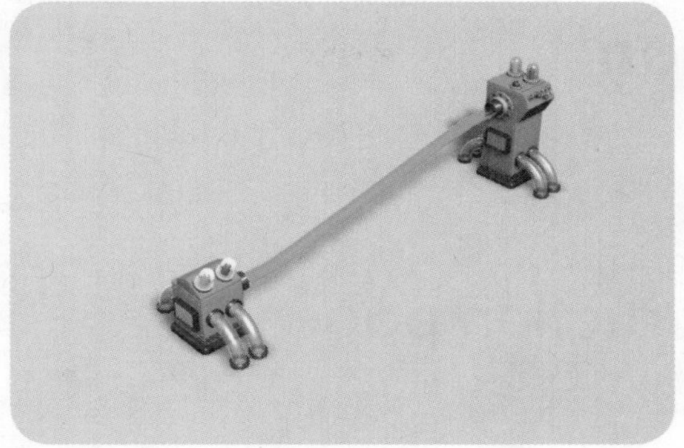

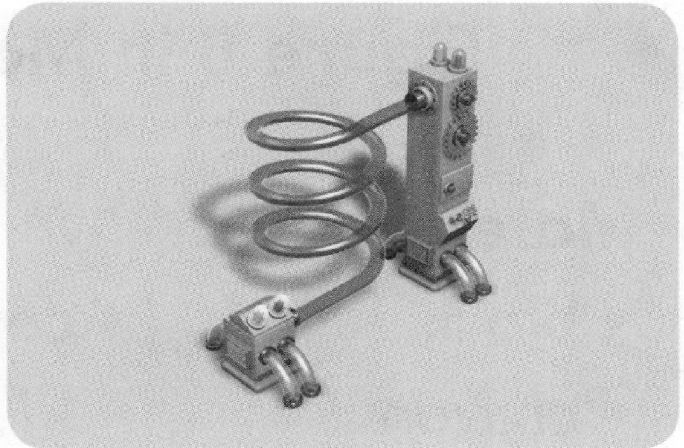

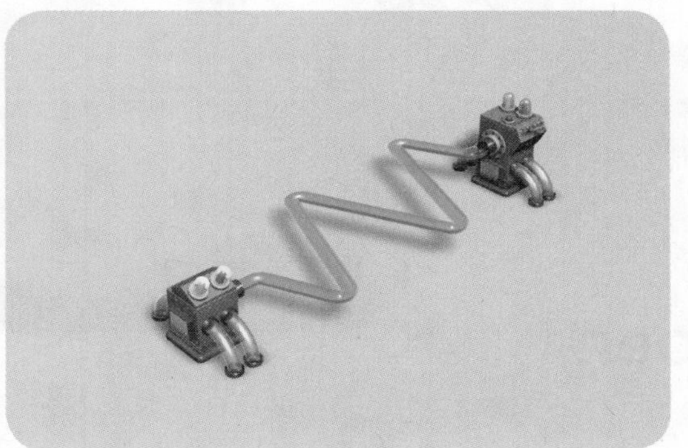

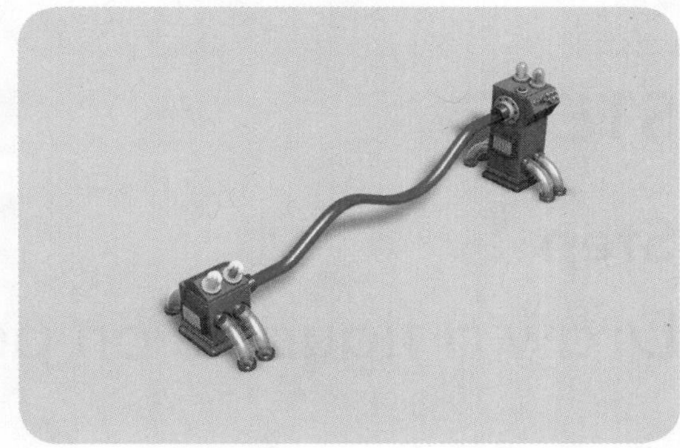

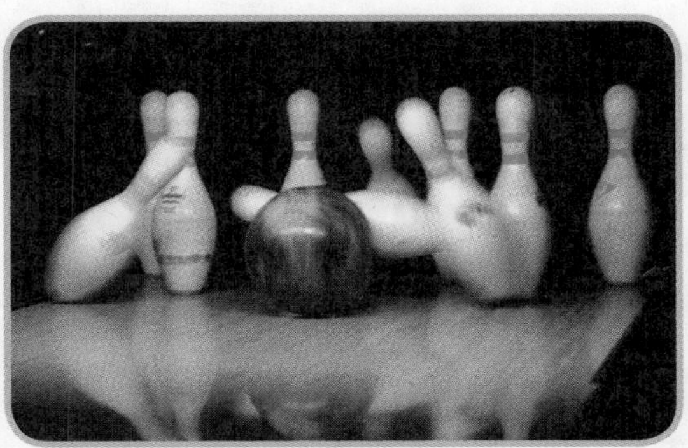

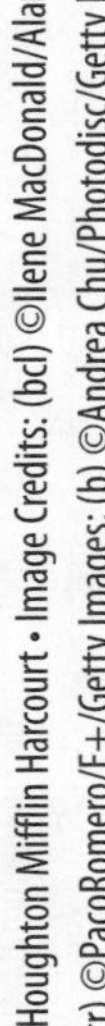

■ Circle the track that changes the direction of the marble to move it round and round.
✱ Circle the pictures of an object changing direction because of a touch.

Unit 2 Performance Task

Figure 8 in Motion

Materials

- block
- construction paper
- crayon

STEPS

Step 1

Draw a figure 8 on paper.

Step 2

Place a block on the figure.

Step 3

Use pushes to move the block so it traces the figure.

Step 4

Keep track of the pushes. How many pushes did it take to complete the figure 8? How many times did you change the direction of the block?

Step 5

Do it again and compare your results.

Check

_____ I drew a figure 8.

_____ I used pushes to move the block to trace the figure 8.

_____ I kept track of how many pushes and how many times I changed the direction of the block.

_____ I did it again and compared the results.

Unit 2 Review

Name ______________________________

1

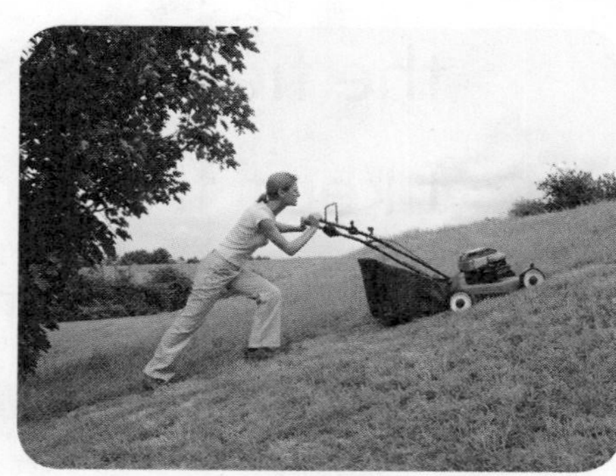

● Which pictures show motion? Circle the correct pictures.

▲ Draw a line between the pictures that show a push. Draw a line between the pictures that show a pull.

3

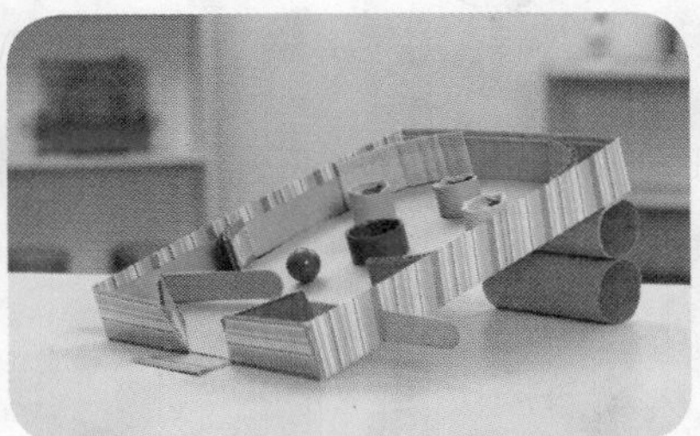

4

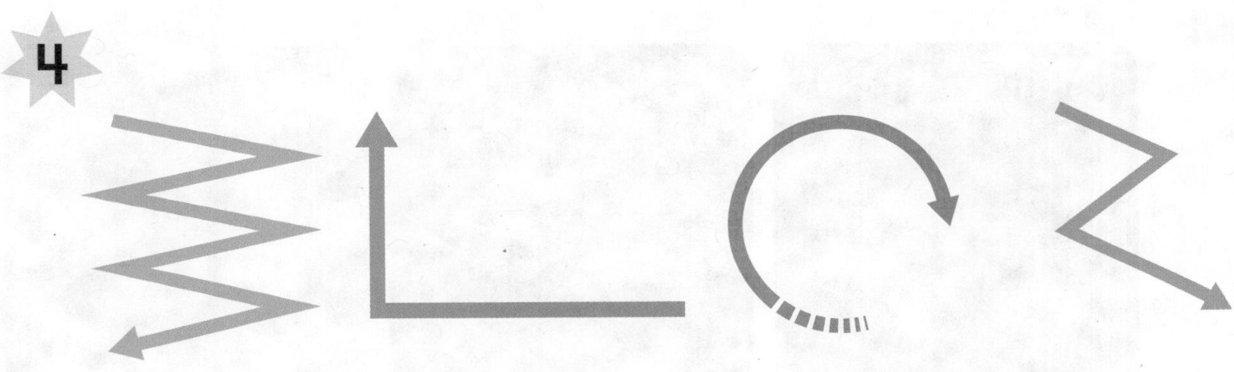

5

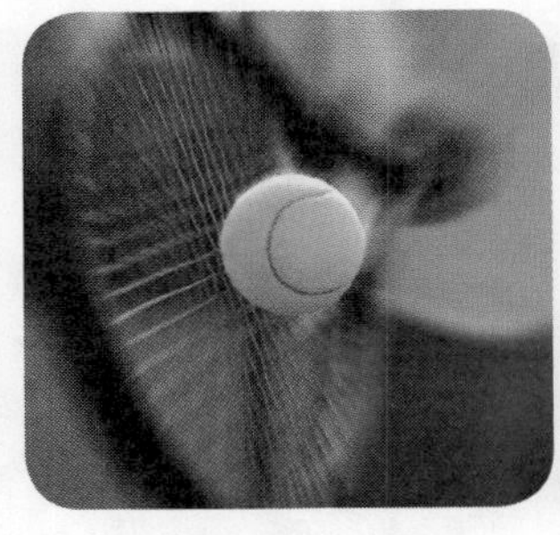

■ Which pictures show how to set up an investigation about how to change the direction of a ball? Circle the correct pictures.

✱ Which arrows show zigzag motion? Circle the correct pictures.

● Which pictures show a force that makes an object move? Circle the correct pictures.

6

7

8

▲ Which pictures show a reason why objects change direction? Circle the correct pictures.

■ Circle the picture that shows the object moving in a straight path.

✱ Which ball will go the fastest? Circle the correct picture.

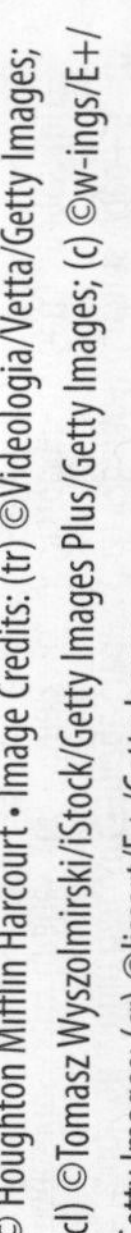

Unit 3
Plants and Animals

Unit Project • Animal Changes
How can you model a way animals change their environment? Investigate to find out.

Unit 3 At a Glance

Unit Vocabulary

living things are alive (p. 76)
nonliving things are not alive (p. 76)
shelter a safe place to live (p. 94)
desert a dry place (p. 108)
forest where many trees grow (p. 110)
pond a small body of fresh water (p. 114)
ocean a very large body of salt water (p. 116)
environment all the things in a place (p. 124)

Vocabulary Game • Guess the Word!

Materials

- one set of word cards

How to Play

1. Make cards.
2. Place cards in a pile.
3. One player picks the top card.
4. The other player guesses the word.

Lesson 1 What Do Plants Need?

By the End of This Lesson

I will be able to tell what plants need to live and grow.

Take It Further

Explore more online.

Soilless Plants

People in Science & Engineering • Dr. Norma Alcantar

Explore online.

Dr. Alcantar studies the gooey stuff inside the prickly pear cactus. She uses it to help clean dirty drinking water.

Draw a line under Dr. Alcantar.

 Draw

▲

• Circle the plant that Dr. Alcantar uses to make clean drinking water. ▲ Draw a picture that shows how Dr. Alcantar's work helps people.

Name ______________________

Lesson Check

Explore online.

The leaves are wilted. What happened? What can help the plant?

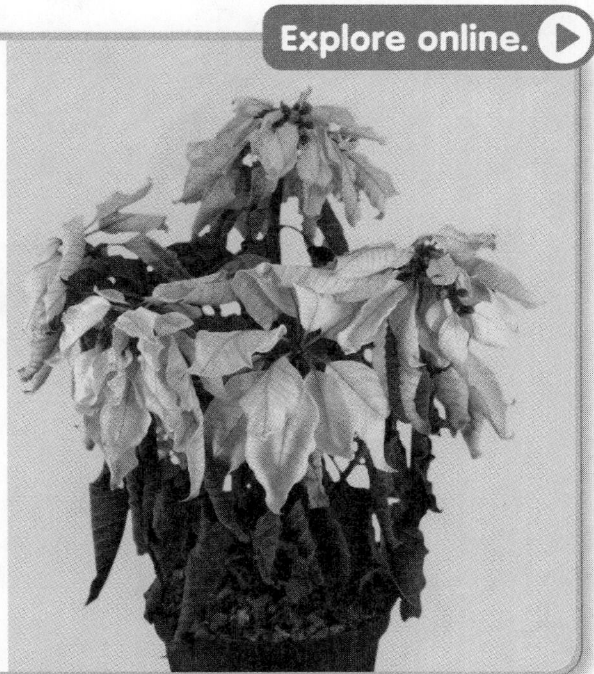

Can You Solve It?

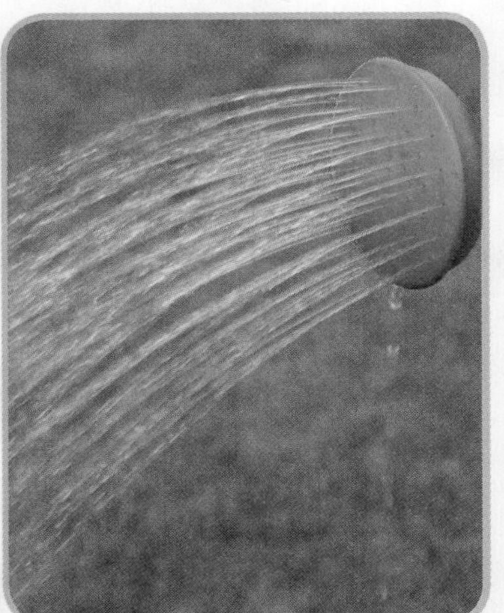

What can help the plant live and grow? Circle the pictures of what you think will help the plant.

Self Check

1

• Circle the living things. ▲ Circle the things plants need to live and grow.

3

4

■ Circle the nonliving things. ✱ Circle the plants that get the things they need to live and grow.

Lesson 2

What Do Animals Need?

By the End of This Lesson

I will be able to tell what animals need to live and grow.

Plants and Animals

Explore online.

Plants need water and light. What do animals need to live and grow?

Can You Explain It?

● Think about what an animal needs to live. ▲ Circle what you think will help the raccoon live and grow.

What People Need

Explore online.

food

water

place to live

air

People need many things to live and grow. They need food and water. They need air. They need a place to live.

Patterns Go to the online handbook for tips. 

Draw a line from the word to the part of the picture the word names.

food

markers

books

water

Apply What You Know **Evidence Notebook**

Patterns Go to the online handbook for tips.

• Circle things people need to live and grow. ▲ List things you need to live and grow. Compare with others. Do you see a pattern? What is your evidence?

What Animals Need

food

water ●

Animals need food and water to live and grow.

air

shelter ▲

Animals need air and shelter.
A **shelter** is a safe place to live.

● Circle the animal getting the food it needs. ▲ Circle the animal in a shelter.

Name ____________________

Hands-On Activity

Pill Bug Home

Explore online.

Materials

How do you make a pill bug home?

Step 1

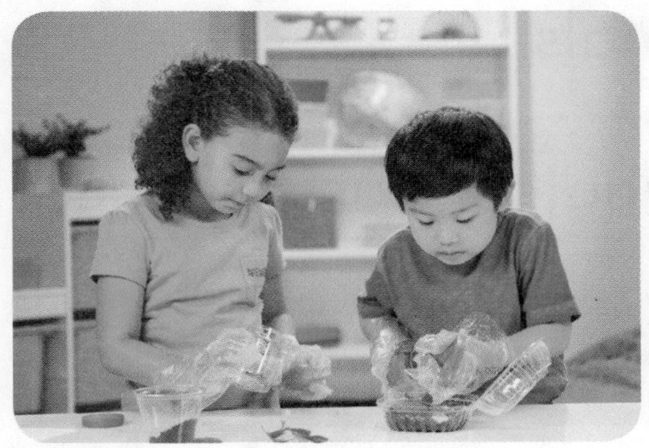

Make a pill bug home. Put all of the objects pill bugs need in the box. Spray the home three times with water.

Step 2

Place the pill bugs in their home.

Step 3

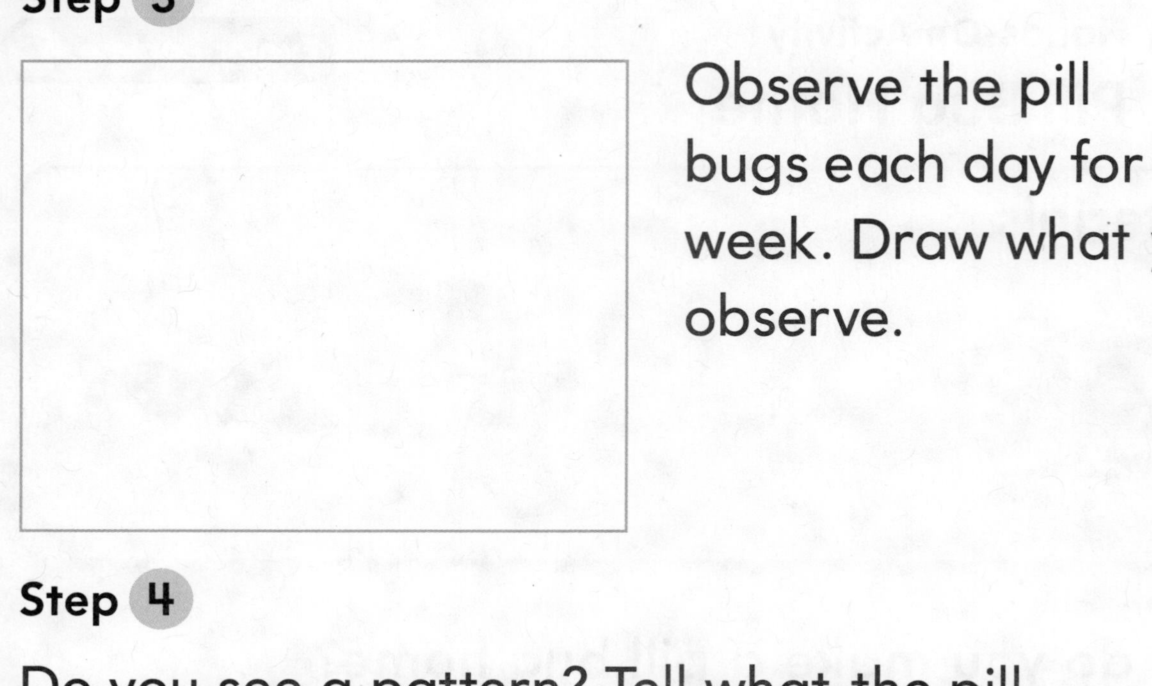

Observe the pill bugs each day for a week. Draw what you observe.

Step 4

Do you see a pattern? Tell what the pill bugs need to live and grow. Describe how they are like other animals.

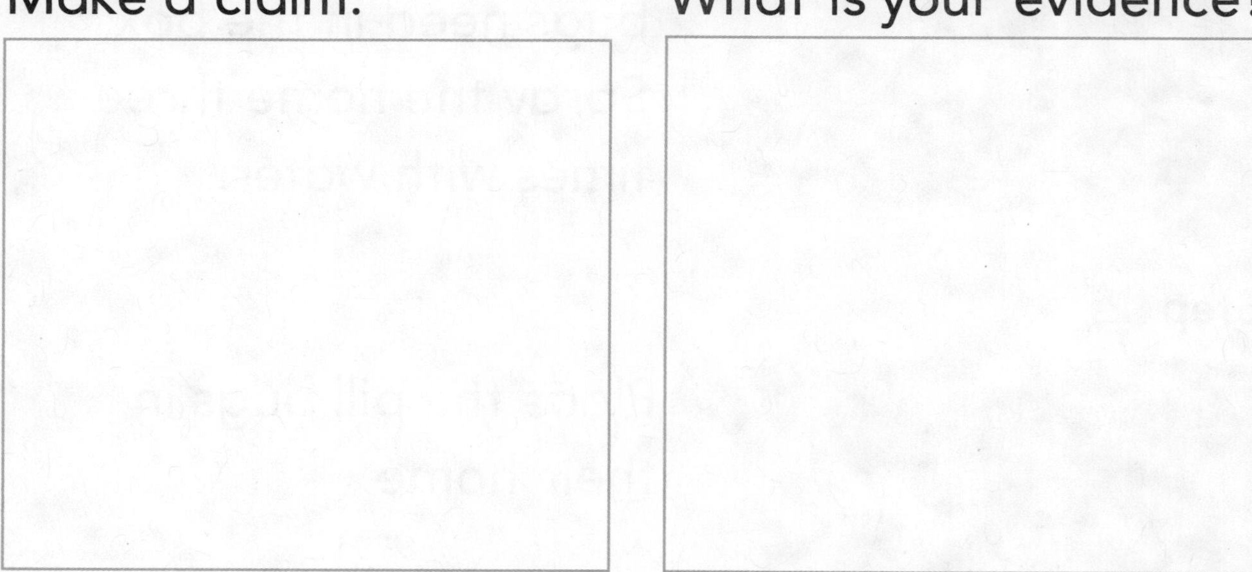

Make a claim.

What is your evidence?

Patterns Go to the online handbook for tips.

Apply What You Know Evidence Notebook

▲

• Circle the picture that shows where the eagle can live to get what it needs to live and grow. ▲ Draw a picture of an animal. Show the animal getting the things it needs.

Water and Air For Animals

Explore online. 

Different kinds of animals use different body parts to take in water.

Analyzing and Interpreting Data Go to the online handbook for tips. 

Do the Math!

Compare Objects Go to the online handbook for tips. 

- Circle the animal that uses its beak to take in water. ▲ Which animal needs to drink more water in a day? Draw a line under the animal that drinks more water in a day.

gills

shark

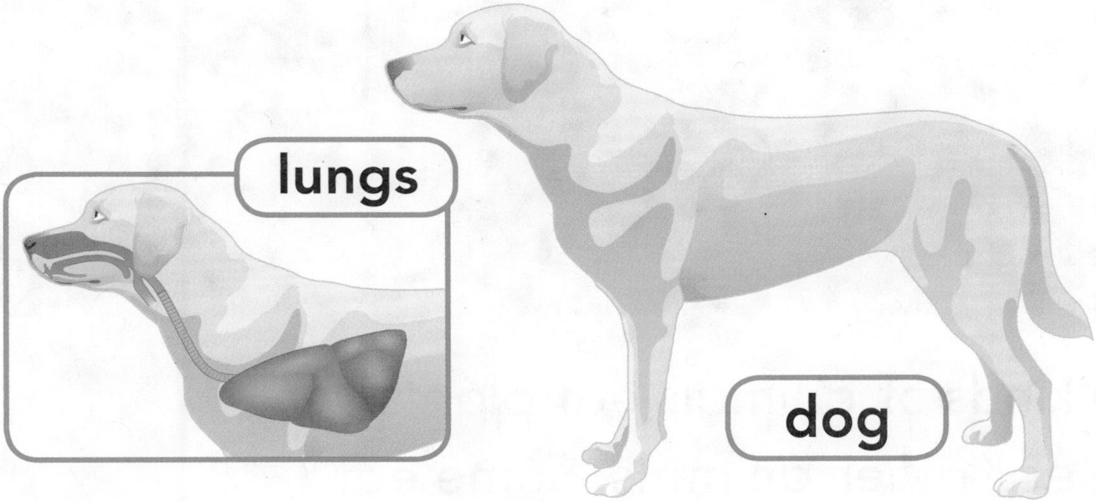

lungs

dog

Animals get the air they need in different ways.

Patterns Go to the online handbook for tips.

Apply What You Know **Evidence Notebook**

- Circle the animal that uses gills to take in air. Draw a line under the animal that uses lungs to take in air. ▲ What body parts do fish use to take in air? What body parts do other animals use? Tell about your evidence.

Food for Animals

Explore online.

hawk

bearded dragons

desert tortoise

Some kinds of animals eat plants. Some eat other animals. Some eat both plants and other animals.

Patterns Go to the online handbook for tips. 

 **Apply What You Know** **Read, Write, Share!** ▲

Research Project Go to the online handbook for tips. 

● Circle the animal that eats only plants. ▲ Work with a partner. Pick an animal. Find out what it eats. Draw a picture of the animal eating a food it likes.

Take It Further

Explore more online.

Wants and Needs

Careers in Science & Engineering • Veterinarian

Explore online.

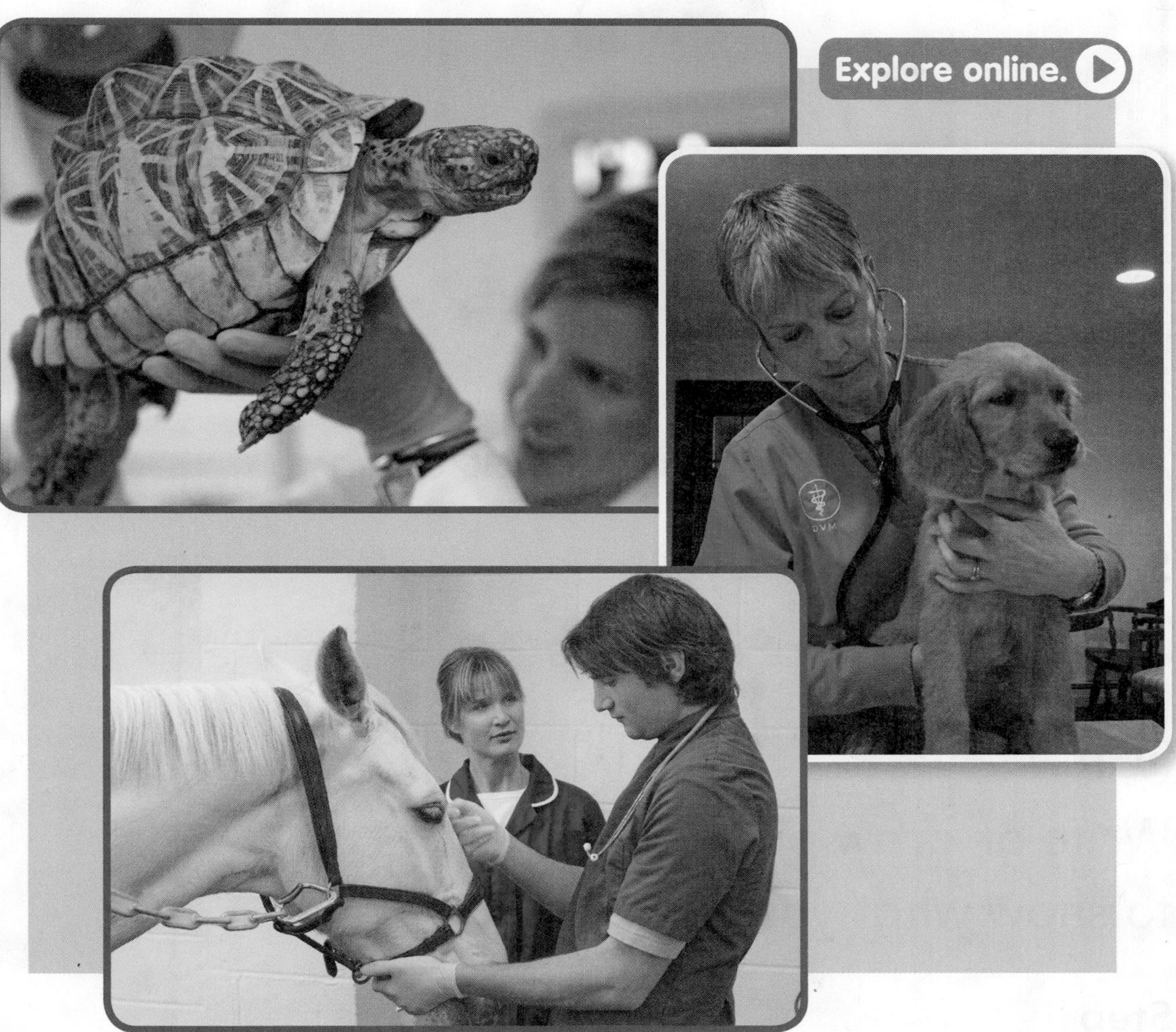

Veterinarians are animal doctors. They take care of all kinds of animals.

Circle the veterinarian working with a farm animal. Draw a line under the pictures that show a veterinarian taking care of a pet.

More about Vets

Read, Write, Share!

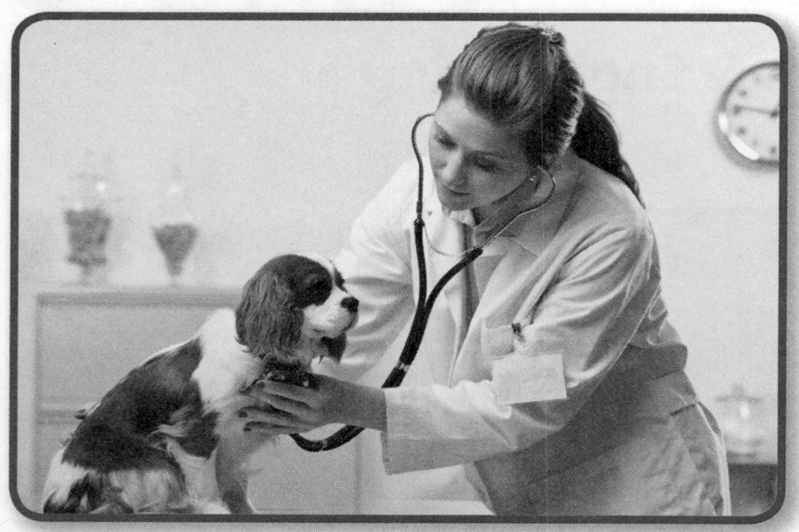

Step 1

Ask questions about veterinarians.

Step 2

Look for answers in books.

Step 3

Write or draw pictures
to show what you learned.

Step 4

Make a poster about veterinarians.
Share it with others.

Research Project Go to the online handbook for tips. 

Name ______________________

Lesson Check

Explore online.

Plants need water and light. What do animals need to live and grow?

Can You Explain It?

● Think about what an animal needs to live. ▲ Circle the things that will help the raccoon live and grow.

Self Check

1

• Circle the animals getting the food they need. ▲ Circle the animals getting the air they need.

3

■ Circle the animals getting the water they need. ✱ Circle the animals that have the shelter they need.

Lesson 3

Where Do Plants and Animals Live?

By the End of This Lesson

I will be able to say why plants and animals live in certain places.

Living Things All Around

Look at the picture. What does the forest have that plants and animals need to live and grow?

Explore online. 

Can You Explain It?

Circle the things that forest plants and animals need to live and grow.

Deserts

Explore online.

A **desert** is a dry place. Each desert is a system. Plants and animals are part of the system. The desert has everything they need to live and grow.

Systems and System Models Go to the online handbook for tips.

Circle each desert animal. Put an X on each desert plant.

desert hare

collared lizard

cacti

sea star

Apply What You Know Read, Write, Share! ▲

Use Visuals Go to the online handbook for tips.

● Circle all the plants and animals that live in a desert. ▲ Draw a desert plant or animal. Tell how it gets what it needs from living in the desert.

Forests

Explore online.

A **forest** is where many trees grow. A forest is a system. Plants and animals are part of the system. The forest has everything they need.

Systems and System Models Go to the online handbook for tips.

Circle each forest animal.

Name ___________________________

Hands-On Activity

Where Plants Live

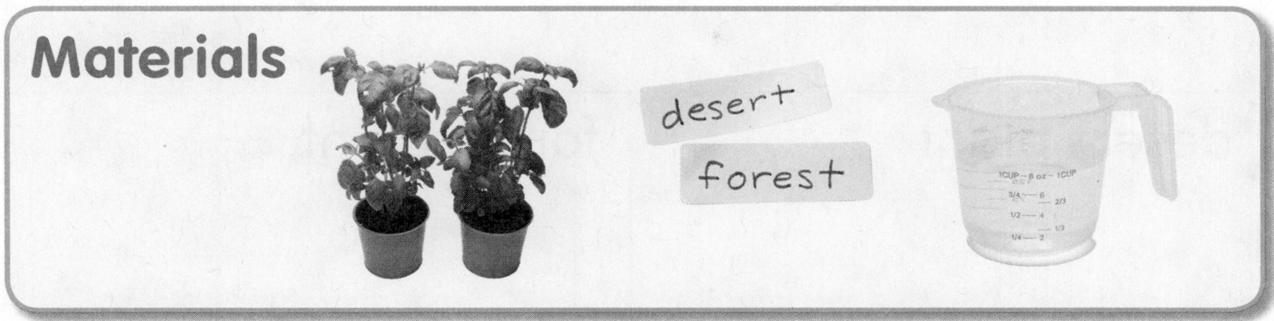

Can a forest plant live in the desert?

Step 1

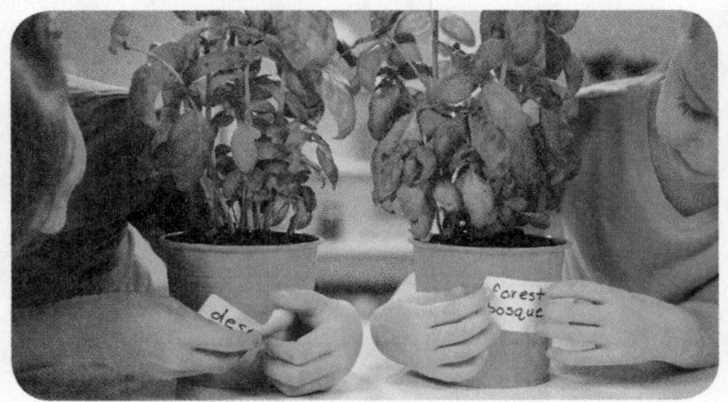

Label one plant "desert." Label the other plant "forest." Put the plants in a sunny place.

Step 2

Water the desert plant once. Water the forest plant every other day.

Step 3

Observe the plants every day for one week.

Step 4

Draw the plants after one week.

desert plant	forest plant

Make a claim.

What is your evidence?

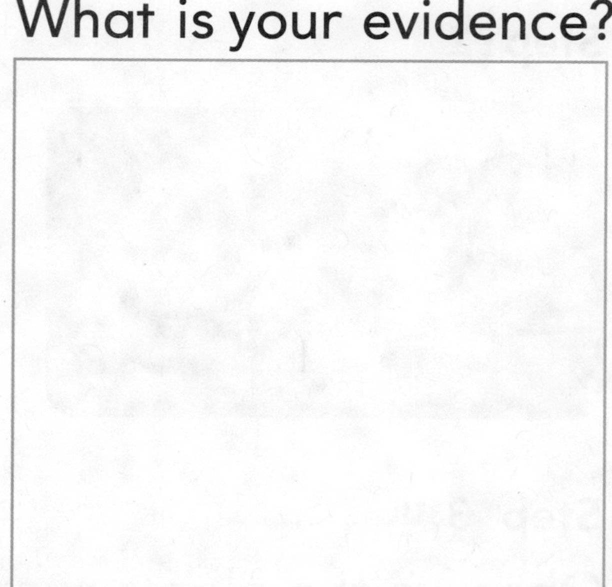

Do the Math!

Trees have been cut down. People want to plant one new tree for each tree that was cut down. How many trees should they plant?

_____ trees

Know Number Sequence Go to the online handbook for tips. 

Apply What You Know Read, Write, Share! ▲

Use Visuals Go to the online handbook for tips. 

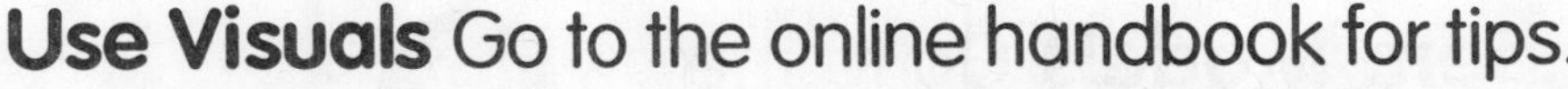

● Write the number of trees people should plant. ▲ Draw an animal getting what it needs from a tree. Use evidence to tell others how the tree helps the animal get what it needs.

Ponds

Explore online.

sunfish

forget-me-not flower

dragonfly

A **pond** is a small body of fresh water. A pond is a system. Living things are part of the system. The pond has everything they need.

Systems and System Models Go to the online handbook for tips.

Circle the pond animal that lives **under** the water.

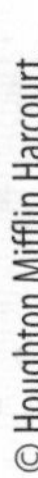

Apply What You Know Read, Write, Share! ▲

Use Visuals Go to the online handbook for tips.

● Circle two pond animals. Put an X on two pond plants. ▲ Make a mobile of a pond. Show the plants and animals that live in or near the pond.

Oceans

Explore online.

An **ocean** is a very large body of salt water. An ocean is a system. Living things are part of the system. An ocean has everything they need.

Systems and System Models Go to the online handbook for tips.

Apply What You Know Read, Write, Share!

Research Project Go to the online handbook for tips.

• Circle the animals in the ocean. ▲ Find out more about the ocean. Pick one plant or animal. Find evidence for how the ocean gives it everything it needs to live and grow.

Explore more online.
Amazon Rain Forest

Take It Further

A Trip to the Zoo!

Explore online.

A zoo designer builds places where animals get what they need.

Circle the animal that gets what it needs from a water area. Put an X on the picture that shows the animal getting the food it needs.

Plan a Zoo

Design a space for a zoo animal. Be sure it can get everything it needs.

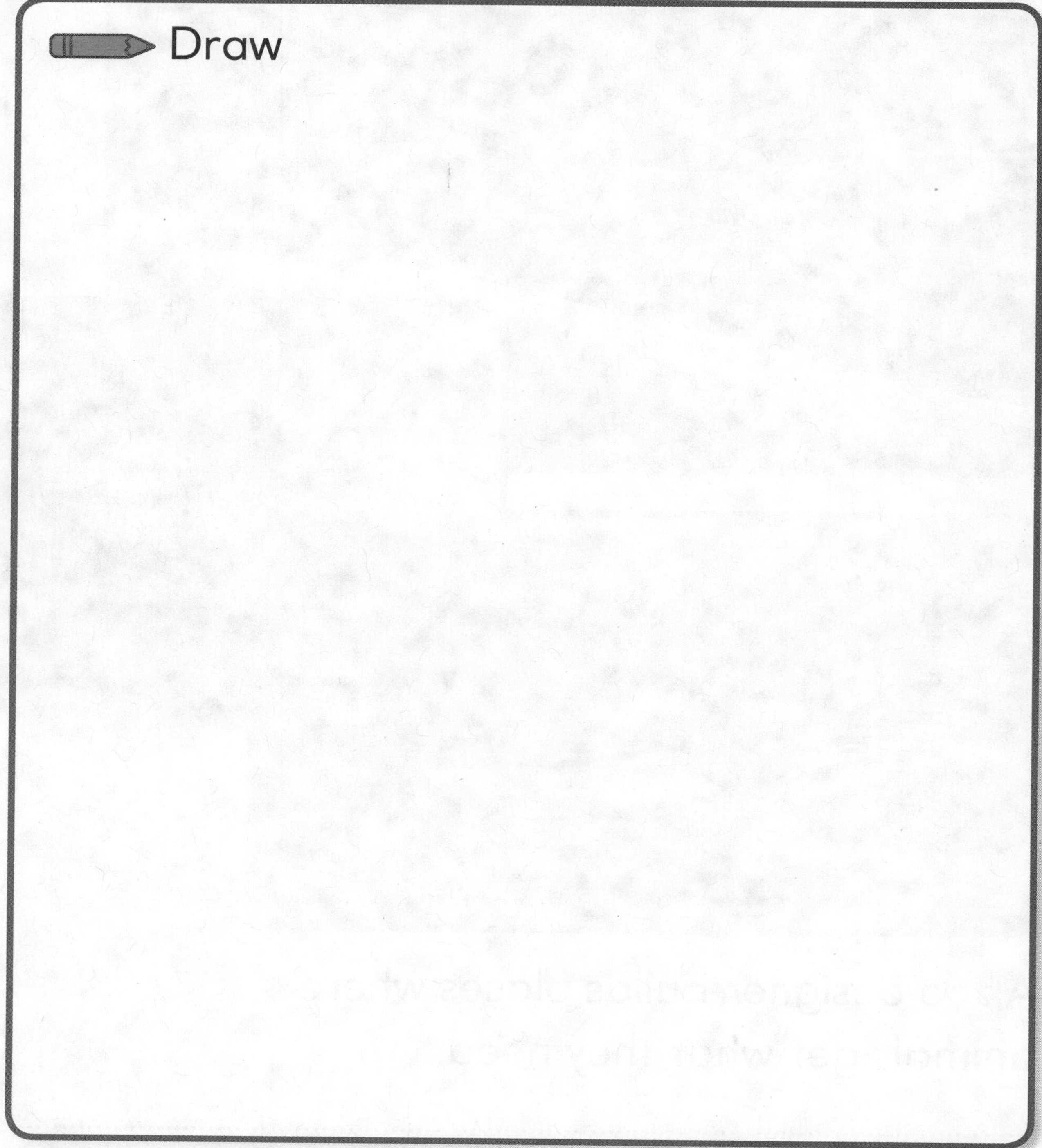

Draw a space for a zoo animal.

Name ____________________

Lesson Check

Look at the picture. What does the forest have that plants and animals need to live and grow?

Explore online.

Can You Explain It?

Circle the things that forest plants and animals need to live and grow.

Self Check

1

● Circle the living things you would find in a forest. ▲ Draw a line from the plant to the place where it grows best.

3

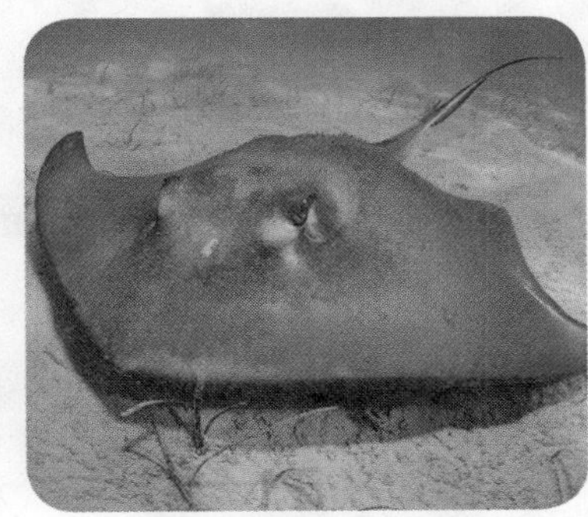

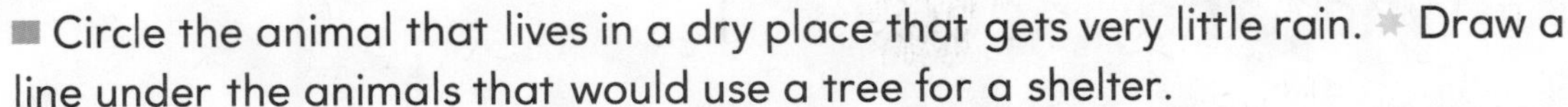

■ Circle the animal that lives in a dry place that gets very little rain. ✶ Draw a line under the animals that would use a tree for a shelter.

How Do Plants and Animals Change Their Environment?

By the End of This Lesson

I will know how living things change the environment to get what they need.

Unit 4
Sun Warms Earth

Unit Project • The Sun Heats Up Land and Water

How hot do soil and water get in the sun? Investigate to find out.

Unit 4 At a Glance

Unit Vocabulary

light is what lets us see things (p. 148)

heat makes things warmer (pp. 150, 160)

shade coolness caused by shelter from the sun's heat (p. 160)

Vocabulary Game • Word Hints

Materials

- one set of word cards

How to Play

1. Make cards.
2. Place the cards face down in a pile.
3. One player picks the top card and gives hints about the word.
4. The other player tries to guess the word.

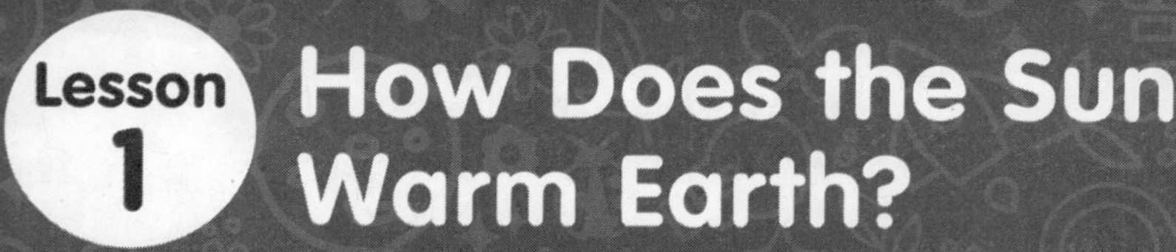

Lesson 1 How Does the Sun Warm Earth?

By the End of This Lesson

I will be able to tell what the sun warms on Earth.

The Sun's Heat and Light

Observe the sun. What things are being warmed by heat from the sun?

Explore online.

Can You Explain It?

Circle the things the sun warms on Earth.

The Sun's Light

Light is what lets us see things.
The sun gives off light. The amount of light from the sun changes throughout the day. This is a pattern.

Cause and Effect Go to the online handbook for tips.

Look at the picture. Draw how the mountains would look during the day.

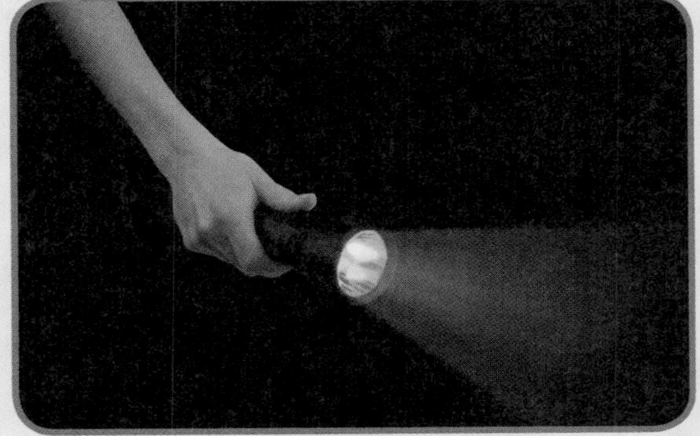

Compare Objects Go to the online handbook for tips.

- Put an X over the picture that shows what gives off light to help us see things.
- ▲ Compare the flashlight to the sun. Circle the one that gives off the most light.

The Sun's Heat

Explore online.

The sun warms land and water. It gives off heat. **Heat** makes things warmer. It can even cause ice to melt.

Apply What You Know Read, Write, Share! ▲

Writing Project Go to the online handbook for tips.

- ● Circle the animal warming itself in the sun.
- ▲ Write a story about a sunny day. Tell about the things you do on a sunny day.

Name ______________________________

Hands-On Activity

The Sun's Heat

Explore online.

How does heat from the sun affect Earth?

Step 1

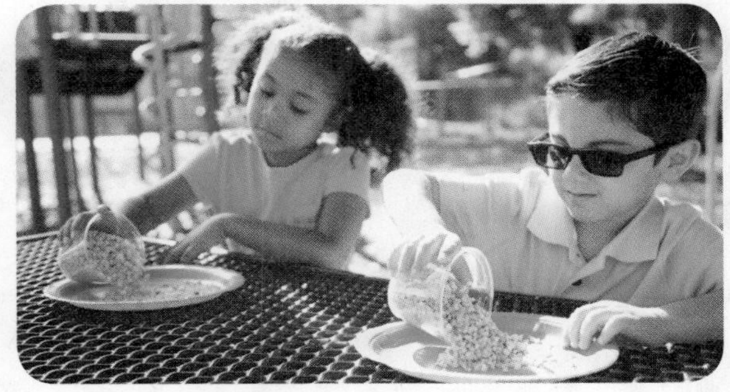

Place a cup of pebbles on each paper plate.

Step 2

Put one of the plates in a sunny place. Put the other plate in a shady place. Wait one hour.

Step 3

Compare and record how they feel. Tell why they feel the way they do.

Sunny Pebbles	Shady Pebbles

Make a claim.

What is your evidence?

Take It Further

Explore more online.

Other Sources of Light

People in Science & Engineering • Galileo Galilei

Explore online.

Galileo studied the sun, stars, and other objects in the sky. He used a telescope to observe them.

Scientific Investigations Use a Variety of Methods
Go to the online handbook for tips.

Circle the picture of Galileo.

Draw

- Draw a picture of what you think Galileo saw when he looked through his telescope.
- ▲ Circle the picture that shows what Galileo used to observe the sky.

Name ______________________

Lesson Check

Observe the sun. What things are being warmed by heat from the sun?

Explore online.

Can You Explain It?

Circle the things the sun warms on Earth.

Self Check

1

● Circle all the places that the sun's light helps you see. ▲ Circle what would help you see things better during the day.

3

■ Circle the glass of water that will warm up fastest. ✱ Circle the pictures of things being warmed by the sun.

Lesson 2 Engineer It • How Can I Protect Myself from the Sun?

By the End of This Lesson

I will be able to tell some ways people can protect themselves from the sun.

Sandbox Problem

Look at the playground. Where is the best place to build a sandbox?

Can You Solve It?

Explore online. 

Draw an X on the place where the sandbox should go.

Heat, Light, and Shade

Explore online.

The sun gives off light and heat.
Heat is what makes things warm.
Shade is coolness caused by shelter from the sun's heat.

Cause and Effect Go to the online handbook for tips.

Circle places in the picture that show where there is shade.

Do the Math!

Which tree would protect you more from the sun?

Compare Objects Go to the online handbook for tips. 

Apply What You Know **Evidence Notebook** ▲

- Circle the tree that would protect you more from the sun.

▲ Work with a partner. List or draw shady places near where you live.

Engineers at Work

Engineers can build things that give shade to protect people from the sun.

Designing Solutions Go to the online handbook for tips.

Apply What You Know **Evidence Notebook**

● Circle the picture of a patio protected from the sun. ▲ Bonnie walks to school every day. The path she walks on does not have any shade. Work with a partner to come up with two solutions that help Bonnie protect herself from the sun. Draw pictures of your ideas.

Name ______________________

Hands-On Activity

Explore online.

Engineer It • Design Shade

Materials

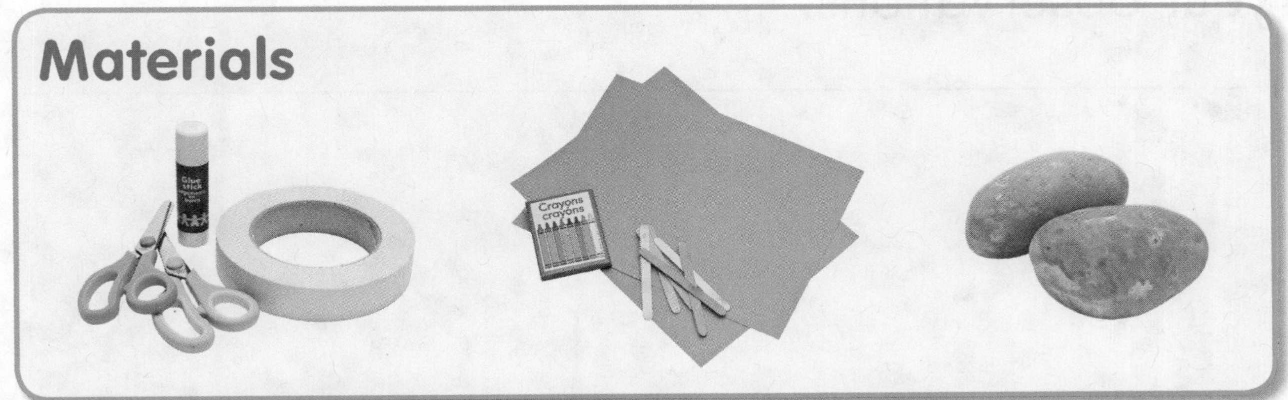

How can I protect Earth's surface from the sun?

Step 1

Design and build a shelter to protect Earth's surface from the sun.

Step 2

Put the shelter in a sunny place. Place one rock under the shelter. Place the other rock in the sun. Wait one hour.

Step 3

Touch each rock and compare. Record your observations.

Make a claim.

What is your evidence?

Take It Further

Explore more online.

Sun Prints

Careers in Science & Engineering • Solar Energy Plant Operator

Explore online.

A solar panel changes sunlight to electricity. A solar energy plant operator makes sure the panels work.

Circle the picture of a solar panel operator.

Read, Write, Share!

Draw

Research Project Go to the online handbook for tips.

Write two questions you have about solar energy plant operators. As a class, use books and the Internet to find the answers. Draw pictures to show what you found out.

Name ________________________

Lesson Check

Look at the playground. Where is the best place to build a sandbox?

Explore online.

Can You Solve It?

Draw an X on the place where the sandbox should go.

Self Check

● Jacob is hot and sweaty. Draw an X on the places he can go to cool down. ▲ Circle things that help block the sun's light.

3

■ Number the pictures from 1 to 3 to show the steps in designing a way to protect the swing set from the sun. ✸ Number the pictures from 1 to 3 to show what happens to a cup of ice when it is put in the sun.

Unit 4 Performance Task

Engineer It • Build a Model Shelter

Materials

- box top
- sand
- chenille sticks
- construction paper

STEPS

Step 1

Define a Problem You want to build a model shelter from the sun on a beach.

Step 2

Plan and Build Use the materials to build a model shelter.

Step 3

Test and Improve Test your design. Does the model provide shelter from the sun? How can you improve your design?

Step 4

Redesign Build a better shelter by making changes to the materials or the way they are used.

Step 5

Communicate Describe how your shelter provides protection from the sun. Explain how you improved your design.

Check

_______ I built a model shelter that provides protection from the sun.

_______ I tested my model.

_______ I redesigned my model so it provides better protection from the sun.

_______ I shared my design with others.

Unit 4 Review

Name ______________________

3

- ● What causes Earth's land and water to warm? Circle the correct picture.
- ▲ What would you see if there were no sun at all? Circle the correct picture.
- ■ Which pictures show evidence that the sun warms Earth? Circle the correct pictures.

5

✱ Which pictures include places you could go to cool down? Circle the correct pictures.

● Where would you put ice if you wanted it to melt quickly? Circle the correct pictures.

6

7

8

▲ Circle the picture that has an X on all the places that provide protection from the sun.

■ Number the pictures from 1 to 3 to show the steps in designing a way to protect the picnic table from the sun.

✱ Draw a line from the picture with little sunlight to the same picture with lot of sunlight.

Unit 5
Weather

Unit Project • Local Weather Forecasts

How accurate is the weather forecast? Investigate to find out.

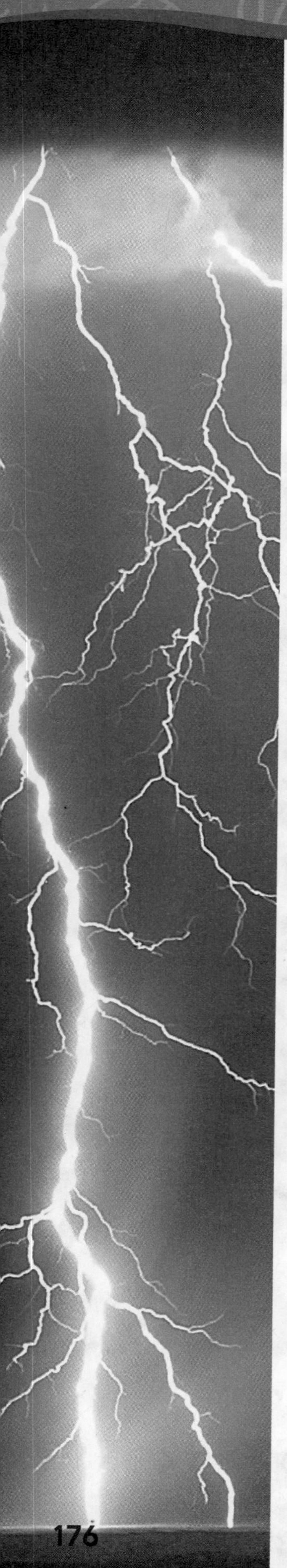

Unit 5 At a Glance

Unit Vocabulary

weather pattern a change in the weather that repeats (p. 181)

season a time of year that has a certain kind of weather (p. 186)

temperature how hot or cold something is (p. 196)

severe weather weather that is very stormy (p. 210)

weather forecast a prediction of what the weather will be like (p. 226)

Vocabulary Game • Act It Out

Materials

- one set of word cards

How to Play

1. Make cards. Place them in a pile.
2. One player picks the top card.
3. The player acts out the word.
4. The other player guesses the word.

Lesson 1 How Can We Observe Weather Patterns?

By the End of This Lesson

I will be able to describe kinds of weather and weather patterns.

Kinds of Weather

Weather can change from day to day. What is the weather like today?

Explore online.

Can You Explain It?

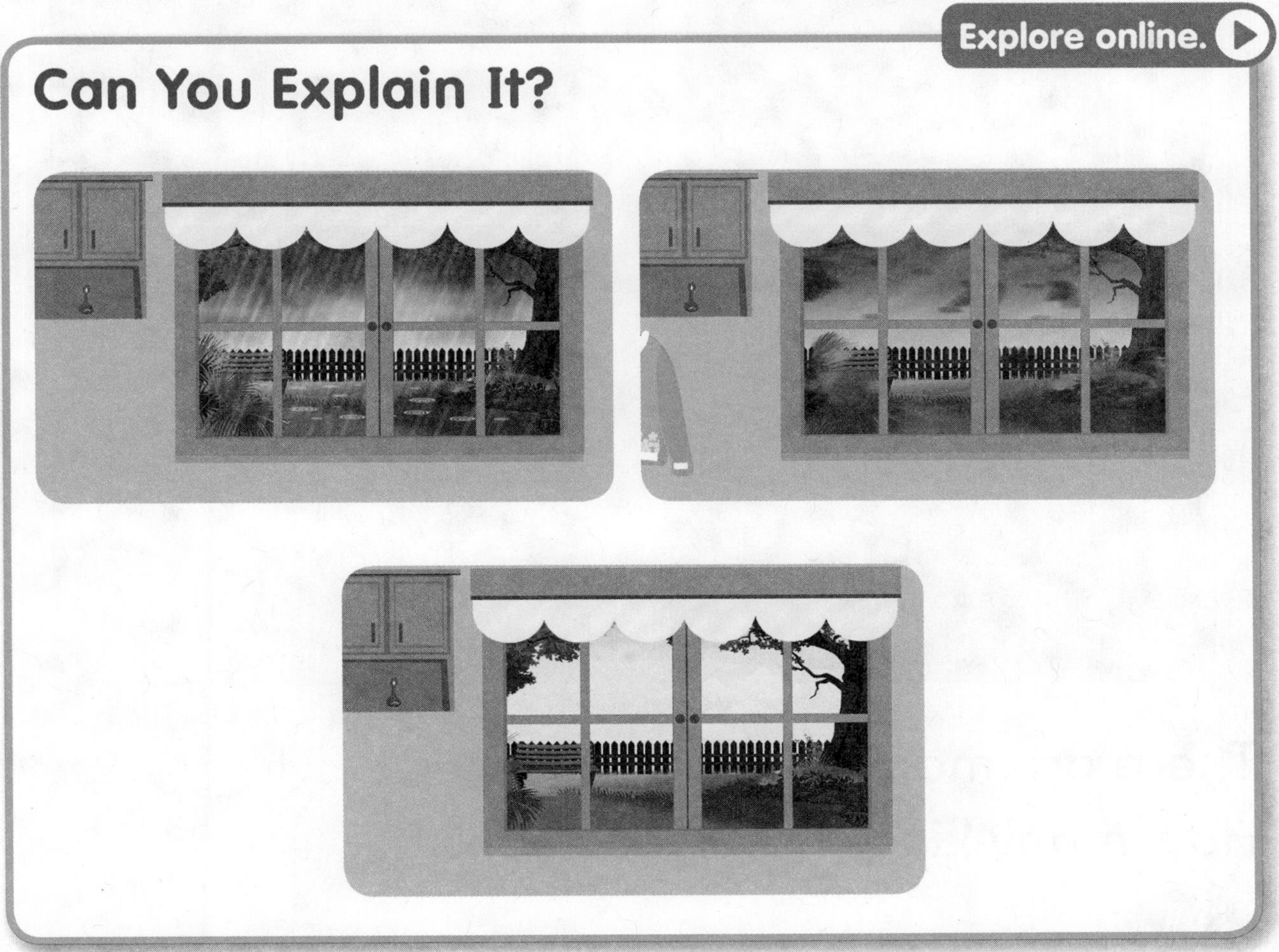

Circle the best weather for a picnic.

Different Kinds of Weather

Explore online.

sunny

rainy

windy

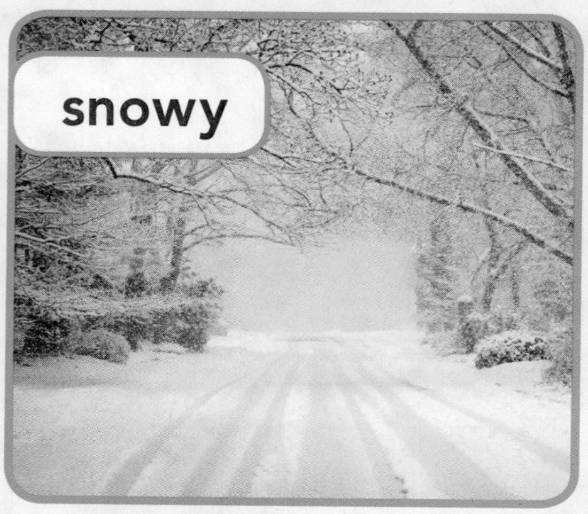
snowy

There are many kinds of weather.

How many kinds have you seen?

Apply What You Know **Evidence Notebook** ▲

Scientific Knowledge Is Based on Empirical Evidence Go to the online handbook for tips.

• Circle all the pictures that show kinds of weather. ▲ Draw yourself on a warm or cold day. Use evidence to explain how you are dressed right for the weather.

Weather Patterns

Explore online.

morning

afternoon

night

A **weather pattern** is a change in weather that repeats. It can be cool in the morning, warm in the afternoon, and cool at night.

Patterns Go to the online handbook for tips. 

Circle the picture that shows the warmest part of the day.

Explore online.

A cloudy day often comes before a rainy day. This is a pattern.

April

Sunday	Monday	Tuesday	Wednesday	Thursday	Friday	Saturday

Classify Objects Go to the online handbook for tips.

• Circle the days in the five-day weather calendar that are part of a cloudy or rainy weather pattern. ▲ Study the weather calendar. Look in magazines for pictures of shirts and shoes you might wear during this month. Cut and sort them into groups. Look for patterns in the weather. Be sure to support your claim with evidence.

Name ___________________________

Explore online.

Hands-On Activity

Observing Patterns in Weather

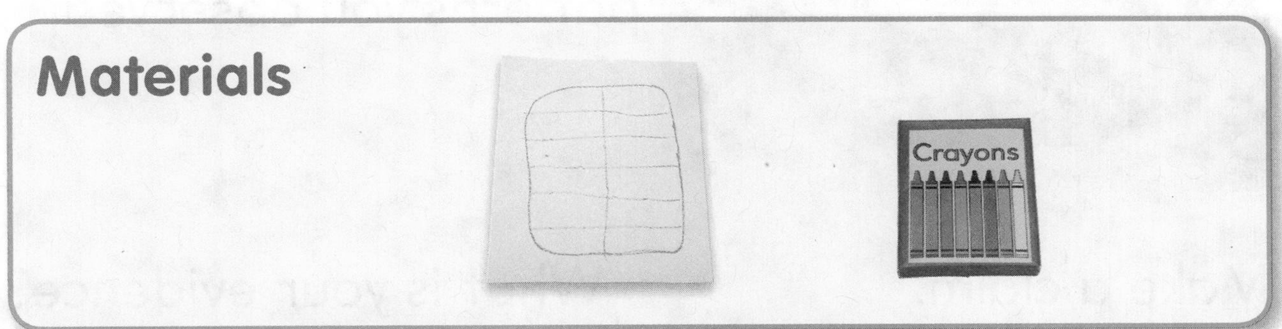

How does the weather change during a week?

Step 1

Observe the weather each day for a week.

Step 2

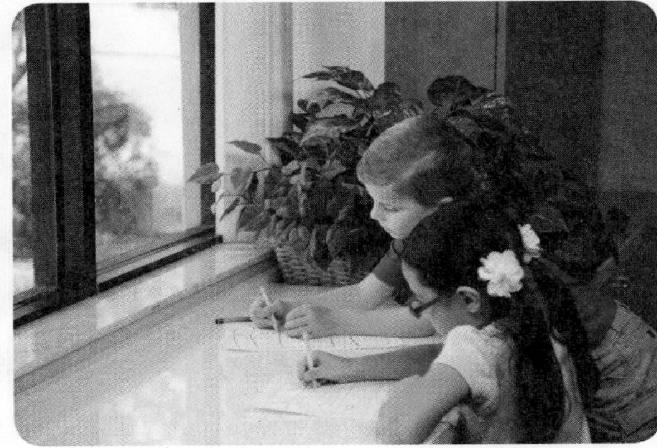

Draw to record the weather on the chart.

Step 3

Look at your chart. Tell about the weather patterns you observed.

Make a claim.

What is your evidence?

Do the Math!

Count the sunny days. Count the rainy days. What kind of weather has more?

May

Sunday	Monday	Tuesday	Wednesday	Thursday	Friday	Saturday

Count and Compare Go to the online handbook for tips.

Apply What You Know **Evidence Notebook** ▲

• Circle the kind of weather that occurred most often. ▲ Watch a weather forecast. Tell about the patterns in the forecast. Talk about the predictions that were made. What evidence was used to support the predictions?

The Seasons

Explore online.

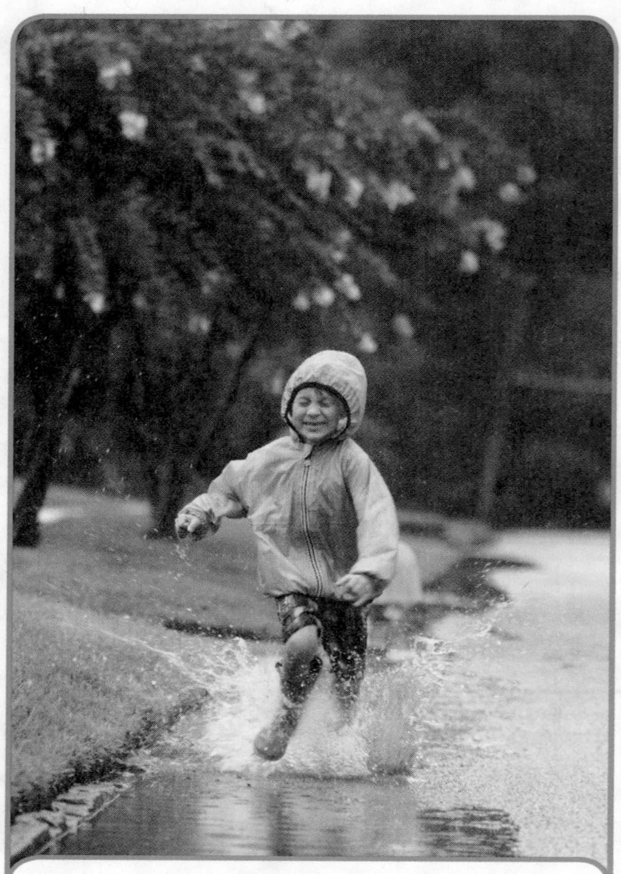

In spring the air gets warmer. Some places get a lot of rain.

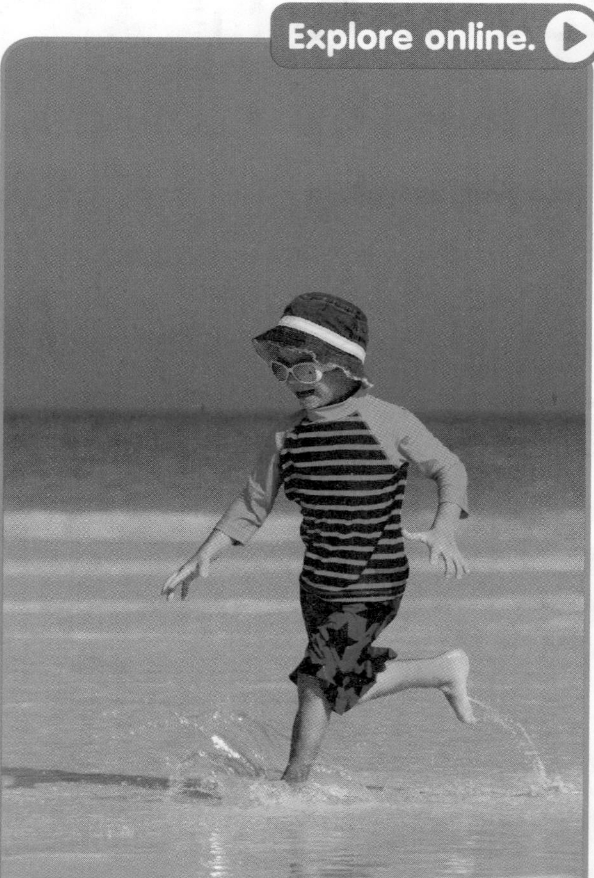

Summer is the warmest season. Summer has the most hours of daylight.

A **season** is a time of year that has a certain kind of weather. A year has four seasons.

Circle the season with the most hours of daylight. Draw an X on the season you like best. Be sure to tell why you like it better than other seasons as evidence for your claim.

Fall has cooler air. In many places fall is a windy time of year.

Winter is the coldest season. Winter has the fewest hours of daylight.

The four seasons are a pattern.

Underline the season with the fewest hours of daylight. Look at the seasons on pages 186 and 187. Put a box around the season it is now.

spring

summer

fall

winter

▲

● Draw a line from the clothes to the season when you might wear them. ▲ Choose a season. Act out something you like to do during that season.

Take It Further

Explore more online.

Extreme Weather

Careers in Science & Engineering • Meteorologist

Explore online.

Current Conditions
46°
WEATHER

5 DAY FORECAST
MON TUES WED THURS FRI

A weather scientist is called a meteorologist. Meteorologists study weather and weather patterns.

Draw a line under the pictures of a meteorologist giving a weather forecast.

More about Meteorologists

Read, Write, Share!

Write or Draw

Writing Project • Inform and Explain Go to the online handbook for tips.

Write or draw your favorite part of a meteorologist's job. Tell how this helps the meteorologist predict the weather. Use evidence to explain your answer.

Name ______________________________

Lesson Check

Weather can change from day to day.

What is the weather like today?

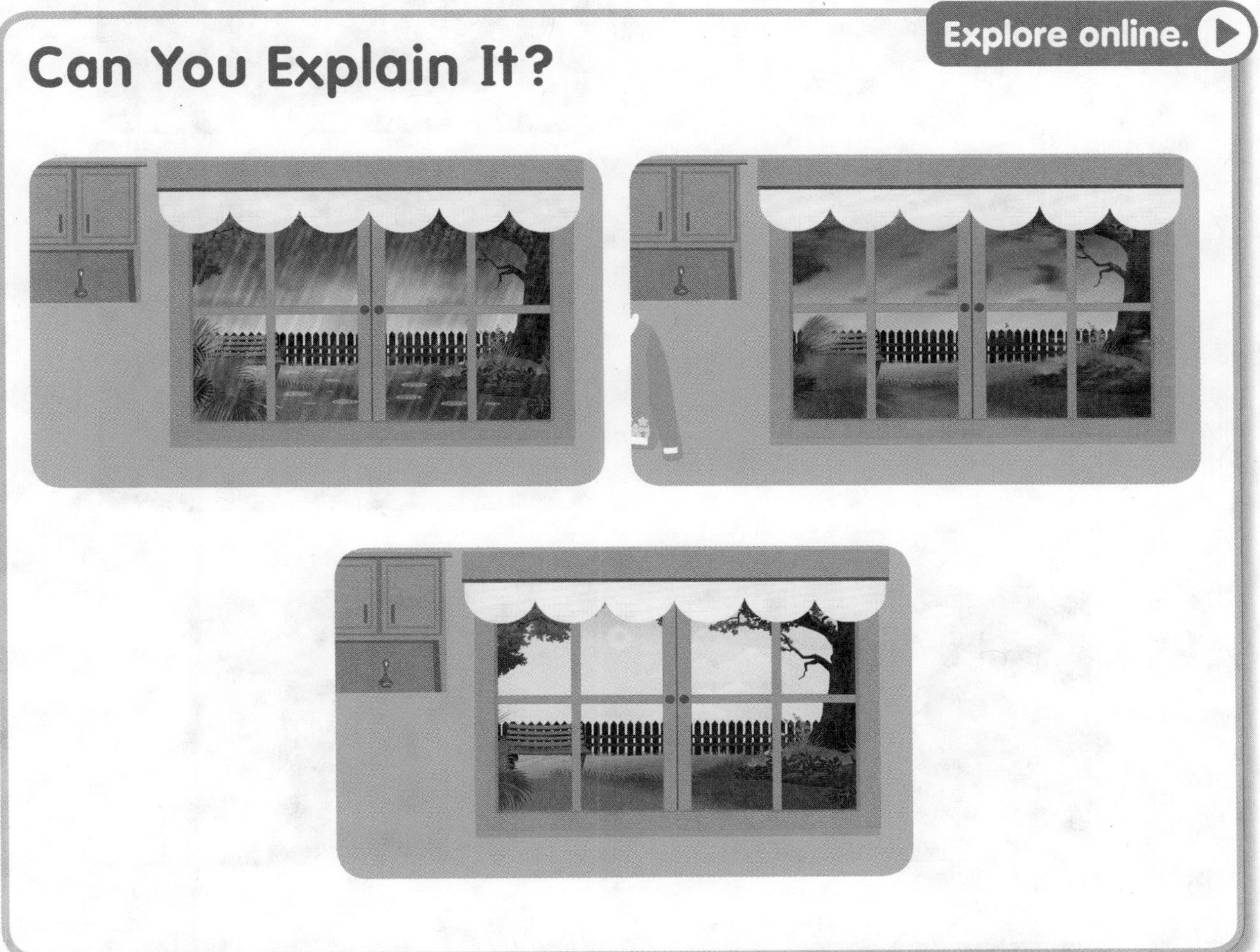

Circle the best weather for a picnic.

Self Check

1

● Draw a line from the weather symbol to the picture that it matches. ▲ Number the seasons from 1 to 4 to show the order. Write number 1 for spring.

3

Monday	Tuesday	Wednesday	Thursday	Friday

■ Circle the pictures that show something you might see when the weather is cloudy or rainy. ✱ Circle the symbol that matches the weather you see more of in this forecast.

Lesson 2

How Can We Measure Weather?

By the End of This Lesson

I will be able to explain how to measure weather.

Measuring Weather

Explore online.

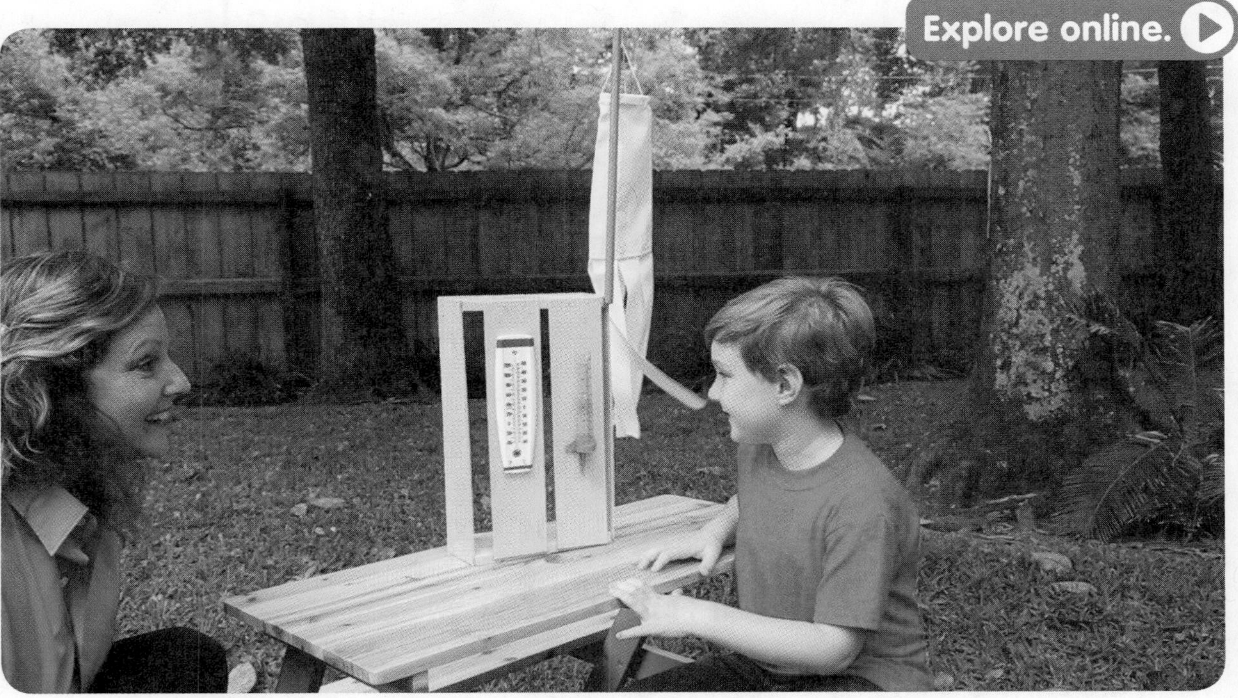

Which tool would help you know if it is a good day to fly a kite?

Can You Solve It?

Circle the weather tool that would help you know if it is a good day to fly a kite.

Weather Tools

Explore online.

thermometers

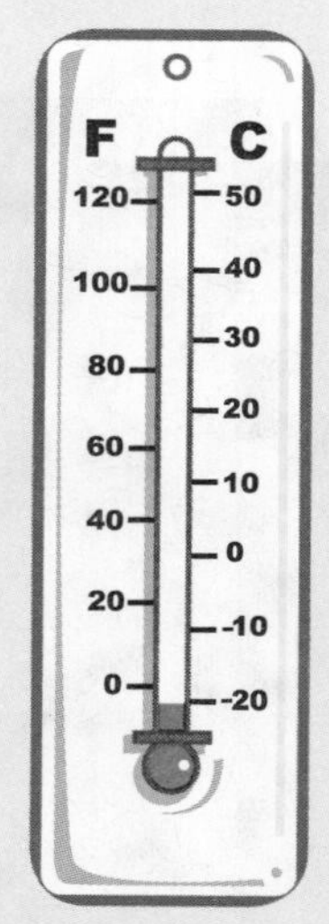

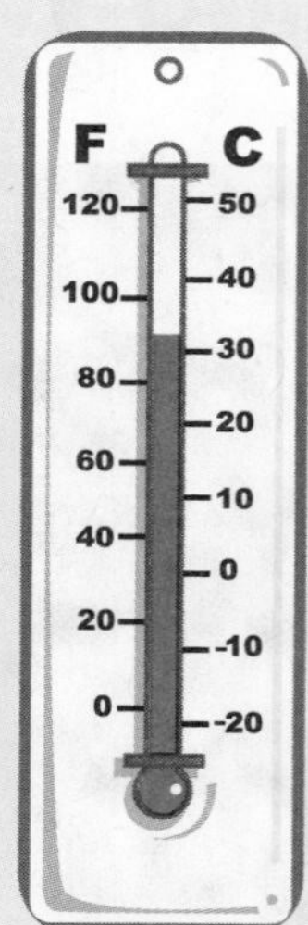

Temperature is how hot or cold something is. A thermometer measures temperature.

A rain gauge measures how much rain has fallen.

rain gauge

▲

● Circle the thermometer that shows the highest temperature. ▲ Draw an X on the tool that measures how much rain has fallen.

Explore online.

windsock

wind vane

N W E S

A windsock shows if it is windy.
A wind vane shows where the
wind is blowing from.

Apply What You Know **Evidence Notebook** 

Patterns Go to the online handbook for tips. 

• Draw an X on the tool that shows where the wind is blowing from. ▲ Observe a thermometer. Now, put it in a cup of warm water and observe how it changes. Then, put the thermometer in a cup of cold water and observe. What happens?

Using Weather Tools

Explore online. 

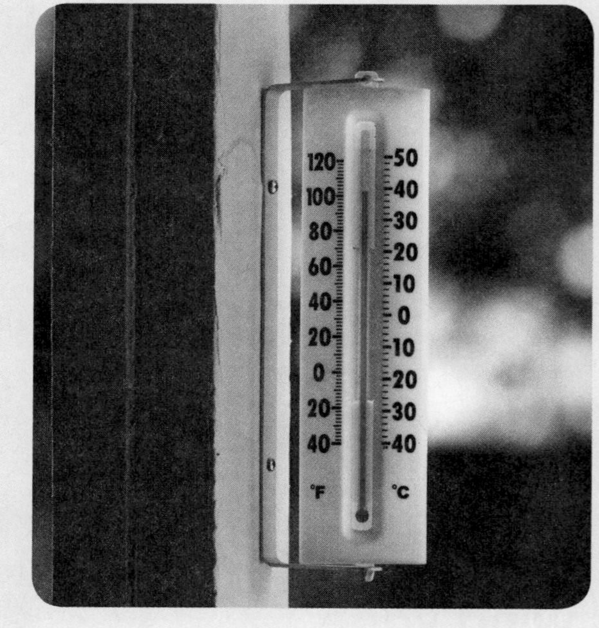

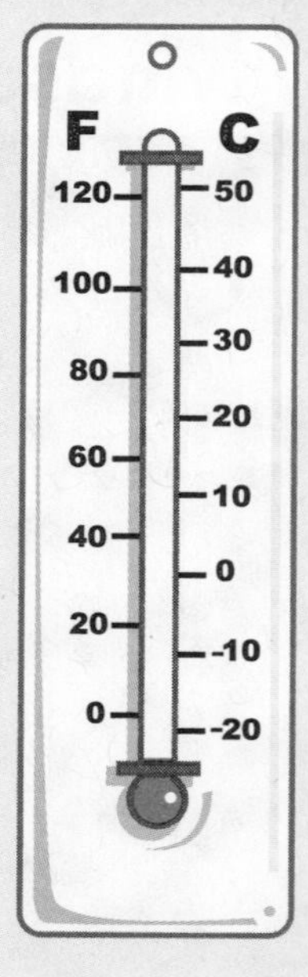

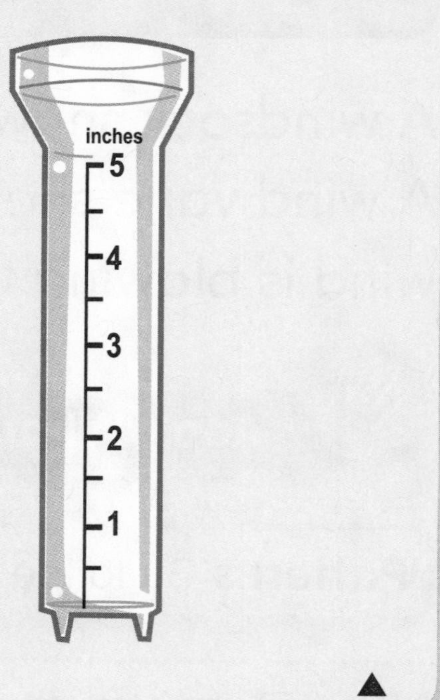

● Color the thermometer to show a hot temperature. ▲ Color the rain gauge to show that two inches of rain fell.

Do the Math!

Draw

▲

Describe Objects Go to the online handbook for tips.

● Circle the windsock on a day that is not windy. ▲ Draw a windsock on a windy day. Tell a classmate about your windsock. Be sure to describe it in as many ways as you can.

Apply What You Know Do the Math!

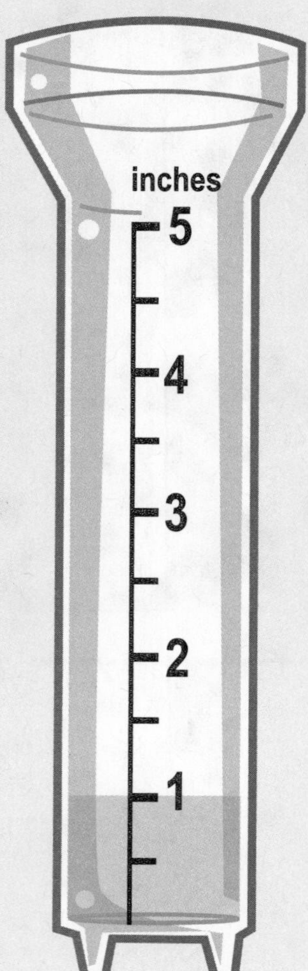

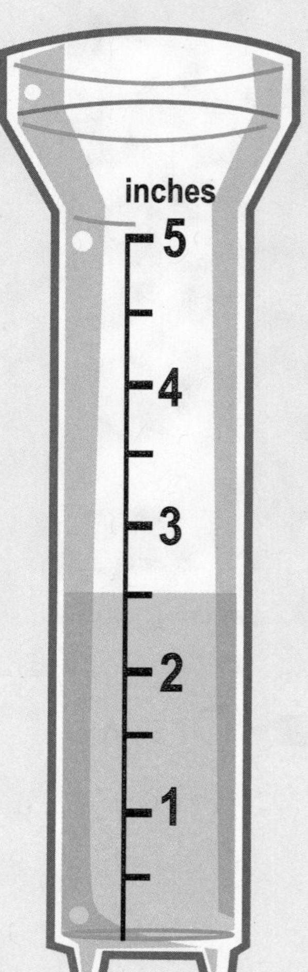

Compare Objects Go to the online handbook for tips.

Circle the rain gauge that has more water.

Name ________________________

Hands-On Activity

Measuring Weather with Tools

Materials

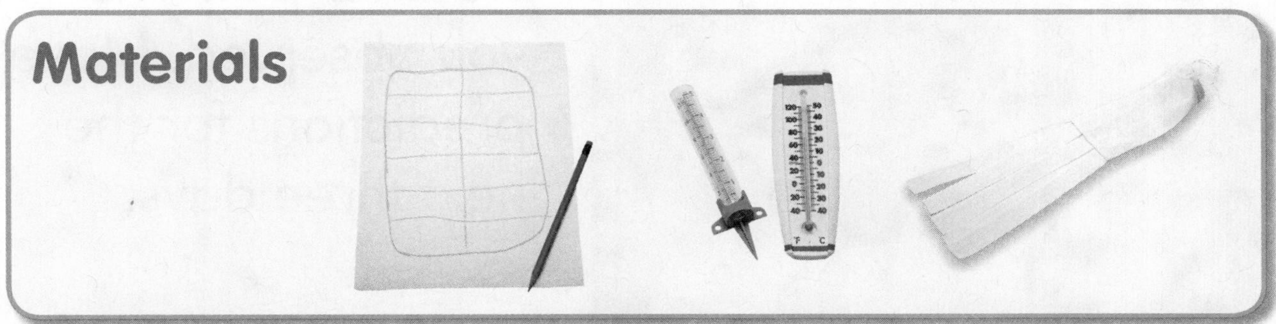

How does the weather change over time?

Step 1

Use the weather tools to measure the weather every day for two weeks.

Step 2

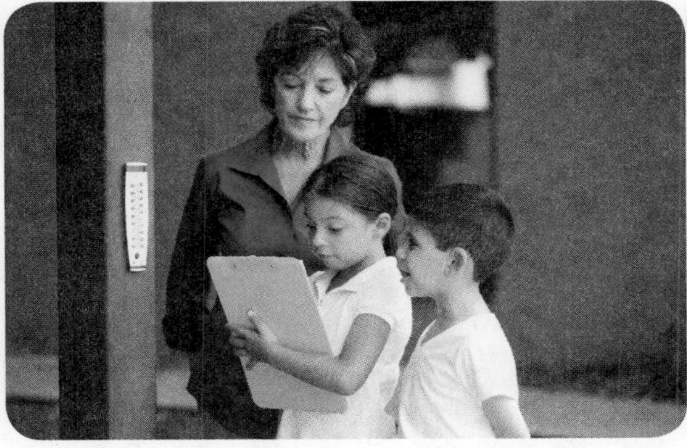

Record your weather measurements on the weather chart each day.

Step 3

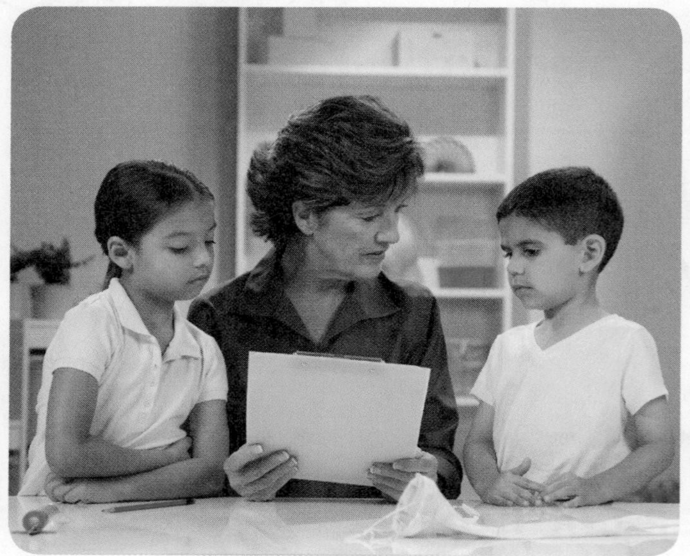

Tell about the weather patterns you observed. Make predictions for the next three days.

Make a claim.

What is your evidence?

Take It Further

Explore more online.

Clouds

People in Science & Engineering • June Bacon-Bercey

Explore online.

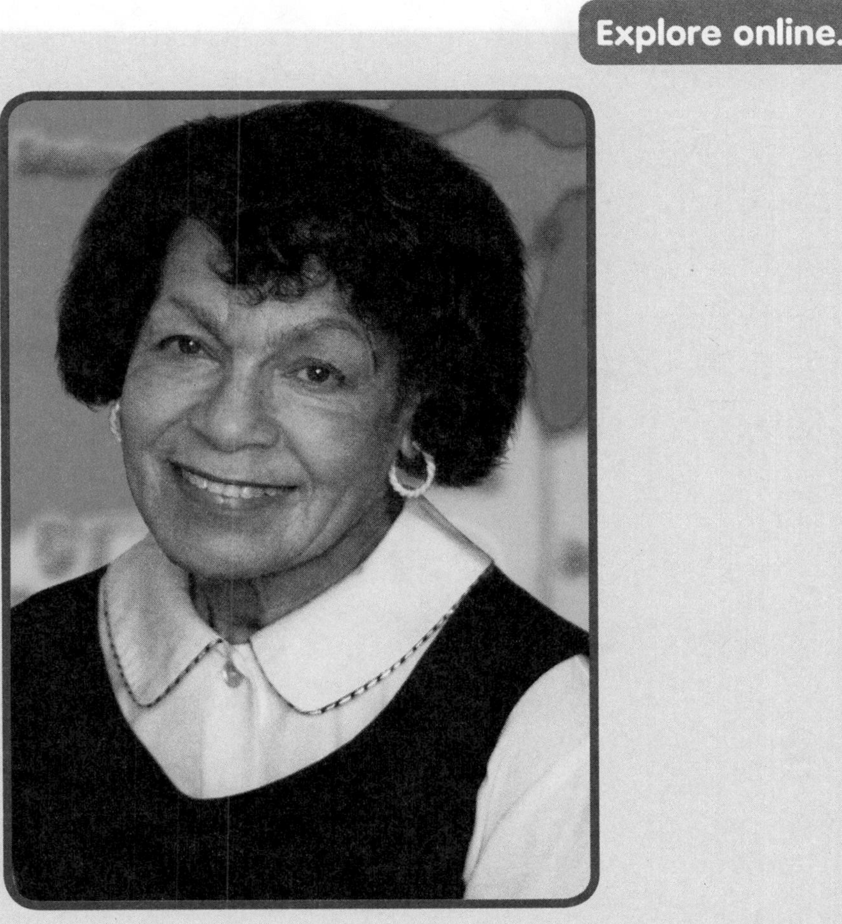

June Bacon-Bercey was the first woman meteorologist on television. She also was a teacher.

Circle the picture of June Bacon-Bercey.

Weather Scientist for a Day!

Read, Write, Share!

Draw

Write to Inform Go to the online handbook for tips. 

Make a report of today's weather. Draw pictures to show if it is rainy, cloudy, windy, snowy, or sunny.

Name ______________________

Lesson Check

Explore online.

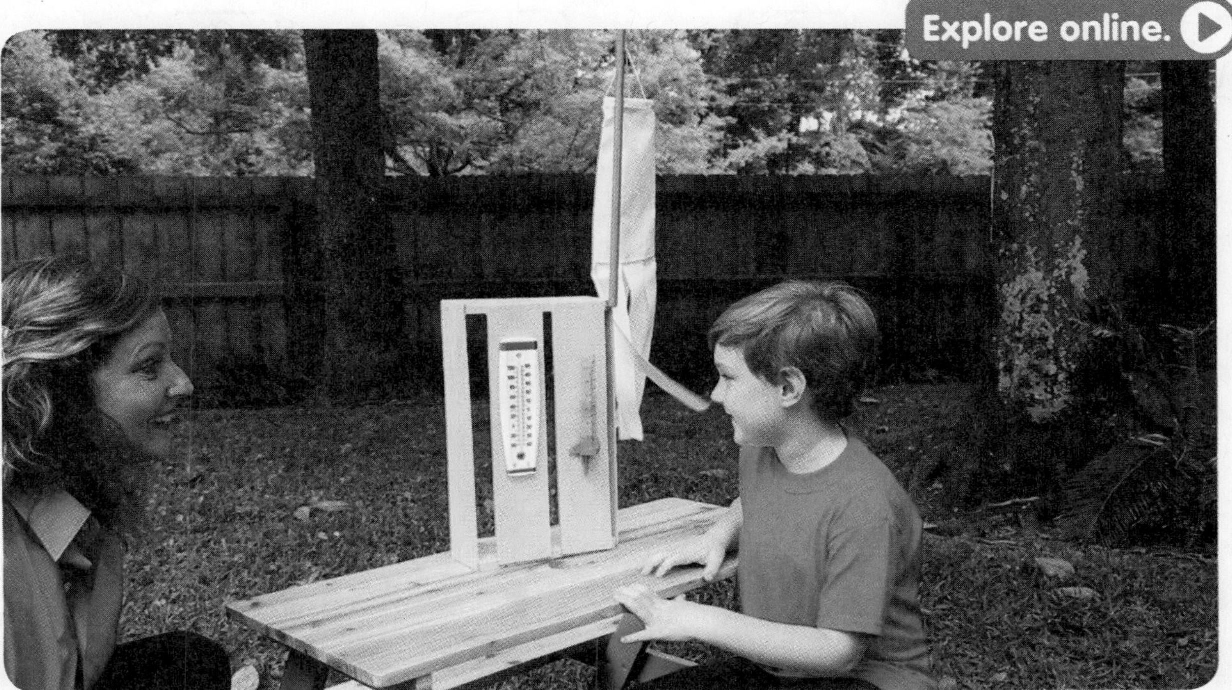

Which tool would help you know if it is a good day to fly a kite?

Can You Solve It?

Circle the weather tool that would help you know if it is a good day to fly a kite.

Self Check

1

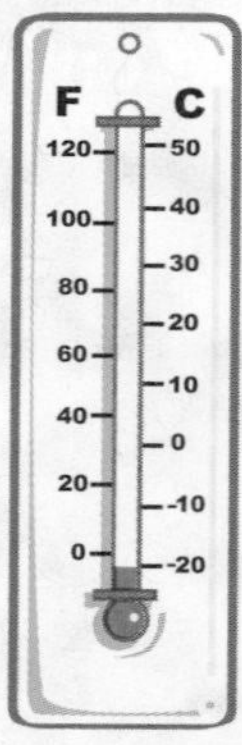

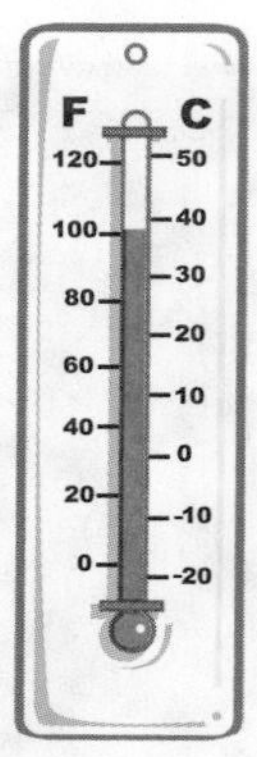

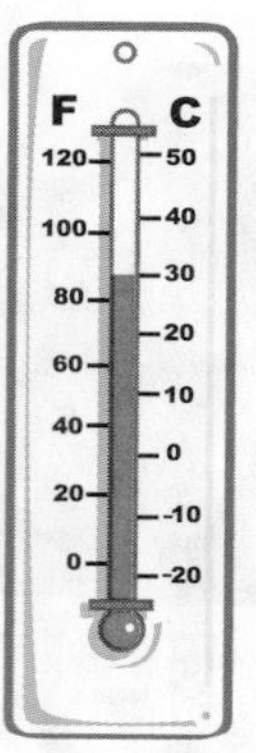

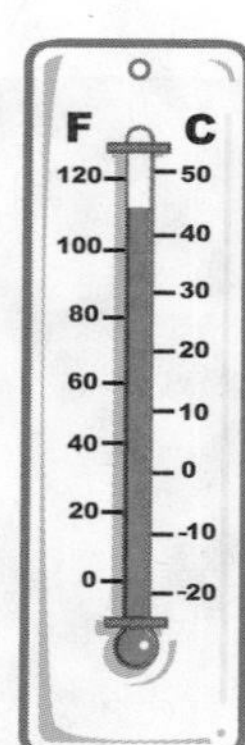

● Circle the pictures that show a pattern of warm weather. ▲ Circle the picture that shows a windy day.

3

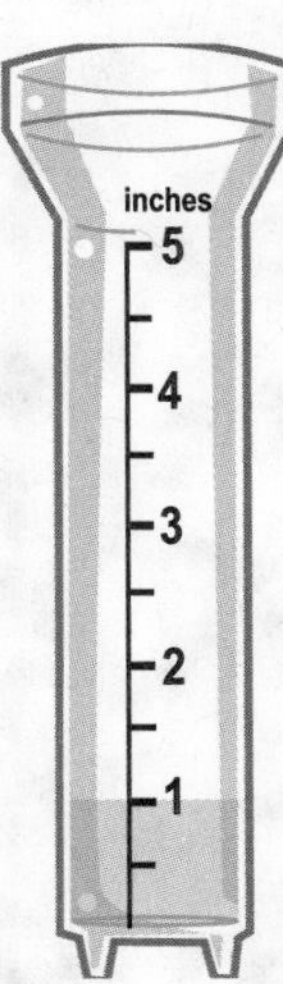

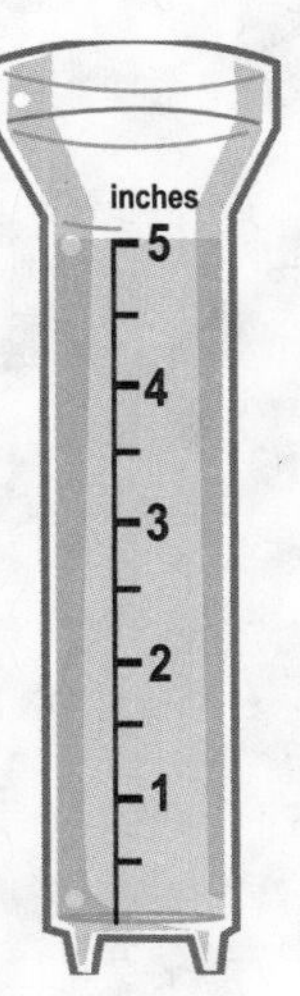

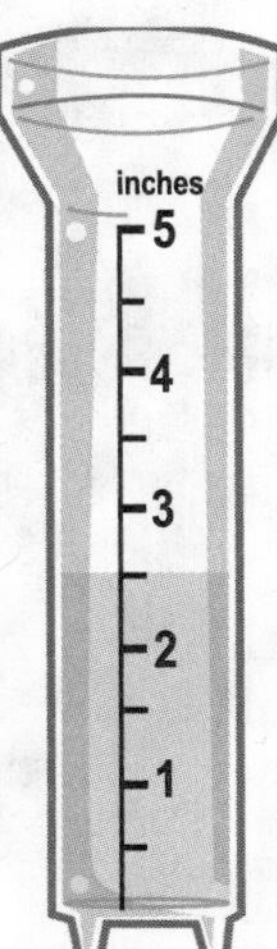

Monday	Tuesday	Wednesday	Thursday	Friday

■ Circle the rain gauge that has the least amount of rain. ✱ Draw symbols in the chart to show a rainy weather pattern.

Lesson 3

Engineer It • What Are Kinds of Severe Weather?

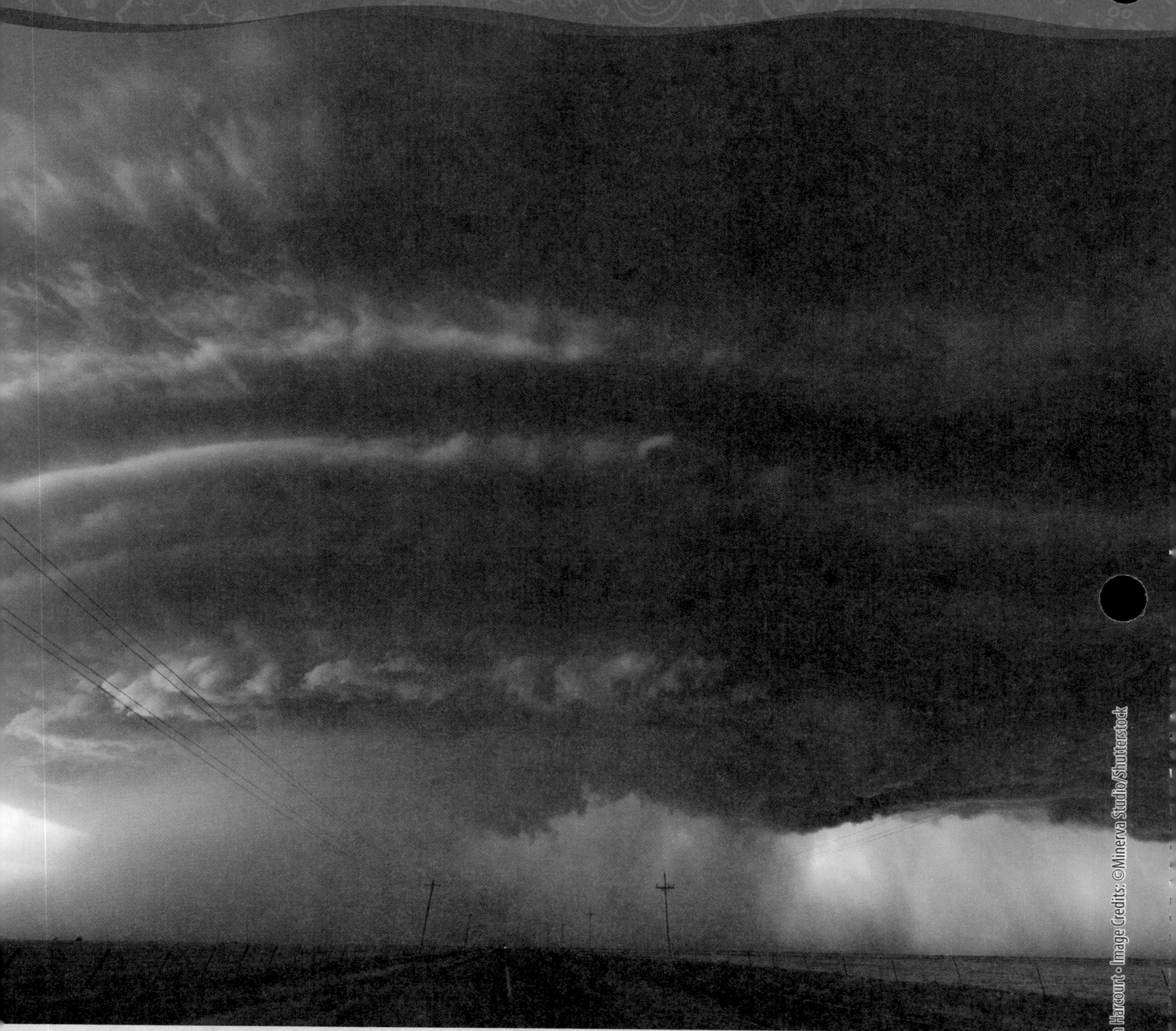

By the End of This Lesson

I will be able to describe patterns for different kinds of severe weather.

Severe Weather

Look at the children playing.

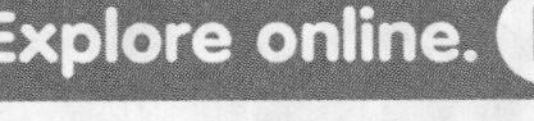

What made them go inside?

Can You Explain It?

● Think about the weather when you play outside. What might make you go inside?

▲ Circle the pictures that show the kind of severe weather that made the children leave the park.

Thunderstorms

Explore online.

Severe weather is weather that is very stormy. A thunderstorm has lots of rain. It also has thunder and lightning. Thunderstorms can happen in places that have warm weather.

Draw an X on the things that happen during a thunderstorm.

Name ______________________________

Hands-On Activity

Explore online.

Engineer It • Model Thunder

Materials

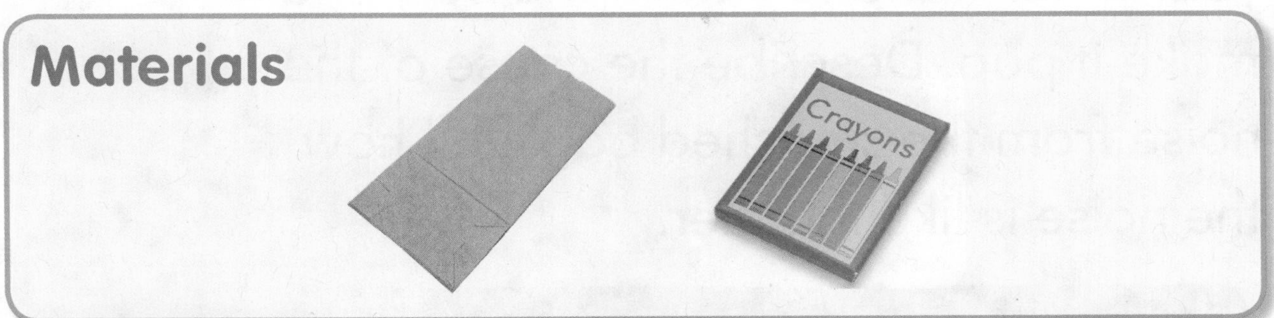

What sound does thunder make?

Step 1

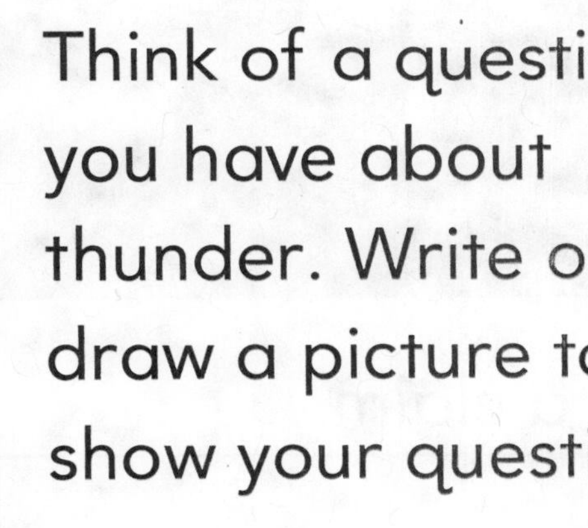

Think of a question you have about thunder. Write or draw a picture to show your question.

Step 2

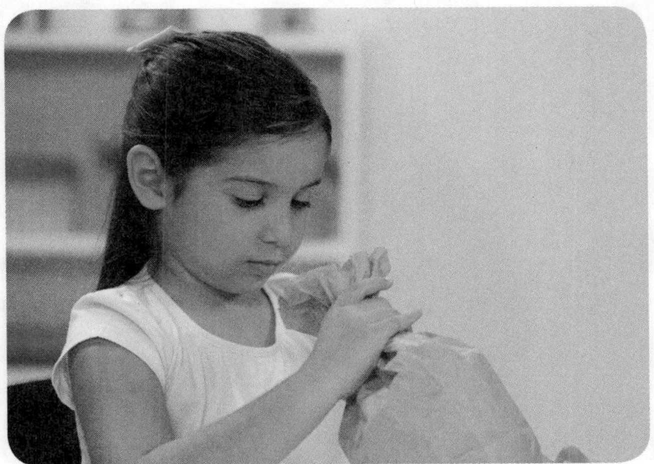

Form a C-shape with your hand, and grasp the paper bag tightly at the top. Blow it up like a balloon.

Step 3

Holding the bag tightly closed, use your other hand to smash the bag and make it pop. Describe the cause of the noise from the smashed bag. Tell how the noise is like thunder.

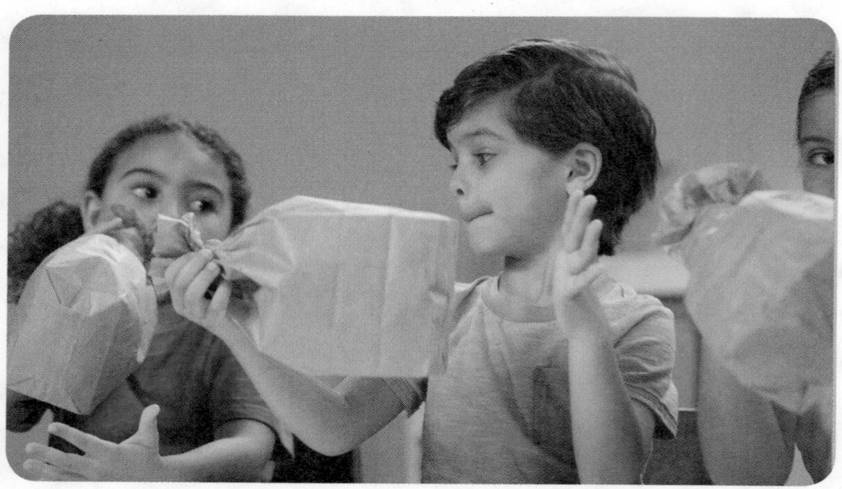

Make a claim.

What is your evidence?

Apply What You Know | Do the Math!

How many days had thunderstorms?

May

S	M	T	W	T	F	S

3   10   15

Know Number Sequence Go to the online handbook for tips.

Circle the number of days that had thunderstorms. Look for lightning and rain.

Winter Storms

Explore online.

A winter storm is a kind of severe weather. The weather during a winter storm is cold. It can be icy. It can be snowy.

Winter storms can happen in places that get cold.

Cause and Effect Go to the online handbook for tips.

Circle the picture of a winter storm with lots of ice.

Evaluating and Communicating Information
Go to the online handbook for tips.

Apply What You Know Read, Write, Share!

Write to Inform Go to the online handbook for tips.

- Look at each picture. Write WS for winter storm. Write T for thunderstorm.

▲ Write a story about a winter storm. Use evidence to support your story.

Tornadoes

Explore online.

A tornado has very strong winds that twist round and round. Many tornadoes happen during thunderstorms. They happen in places where cold air and warm air meet.

Apply What You Know Read, Write, Share! ▲

Ask Questions Go to the online handbook for tips.

● Circle a tornado touching the ground. ▲ Think of questions you have about tornadoes. Work with a partner to find the answers. Share what you learn.

Hurricanes

Explore online.

Hurricanes happen close to an ocean. They can have strong winds, rain and make large waves.

Cause and Effect Go to the online handbook for tips. 

Draw an X on the part of the picture that shows where a hurricane forms.

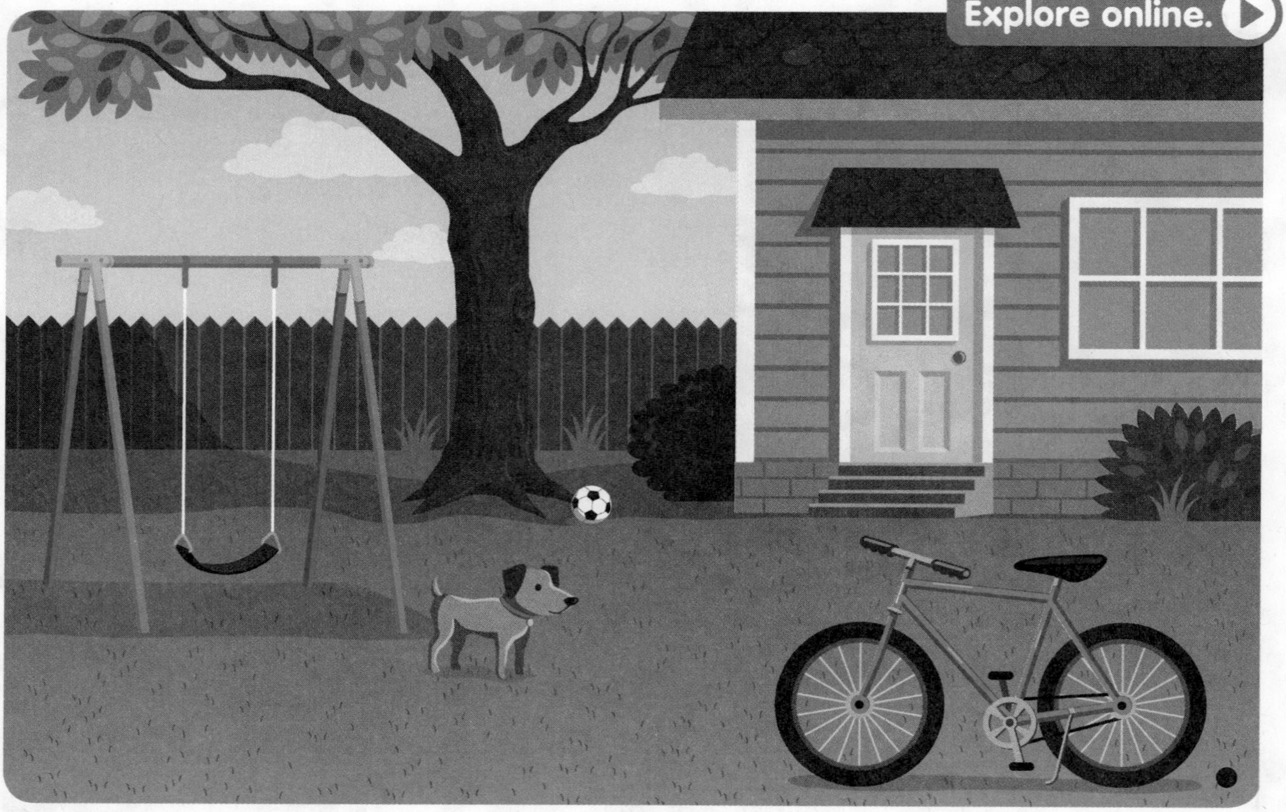

Explore online.

Cause and Effect Go to the online handbook for tips. 

● Circle the objects you should bring in when a hurricane is coming. ▲ How are hurricanes and tornadoes alike and different? Use evidence to support your ideas. Share ideas with a friend.

Take It Further

Explore more online.

Make a Twisty Tornado

Dust Storms

Explore online.

Dust storms happen in deserts and in dry flat places. Strong winds form a large cloud of sand and soil.

Draw an X on the picture where it looks like a dust storm is starting.

Draw

Draw a picture of what the city will look like after a dust storm.

Name ____________________

Lesson Check

Look at the children playing.

Explore online.

What made them go inside?

Can You Explain It?

● Think about the weather when you play outside. What might make you go inside?
▲ Circle the pictures that show the kind of severe weather that made the children leave the park.

Self Check

1

● Maggie saw a tornado near her home. Circle the picture that shows what Maggie saw.
▲ Jessie took pictures of a winter storm. Number the pictures to show what happened at the beginning, middle, and end of the winter storm.

3

4

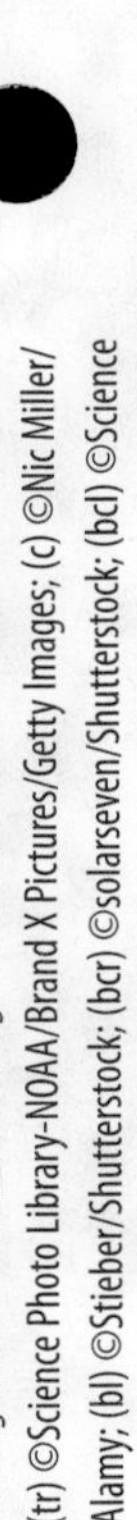

■ Circle the picture that shows the kind of severe weather that happens over warm ocean water. ✱ Circle the kinds of severe weather that have strong winds.

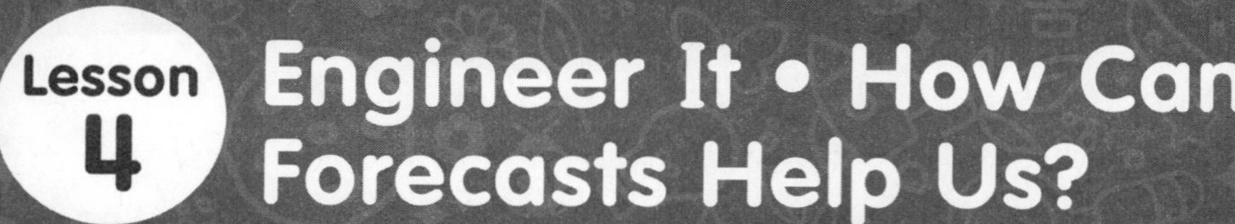

Lesson 4 Engineer It • How Can Forecasts Help Us?

By the End of This Lesson

I will be able to explain how to get ready for severe weather.

Plan for Severe Weather

Explore online.

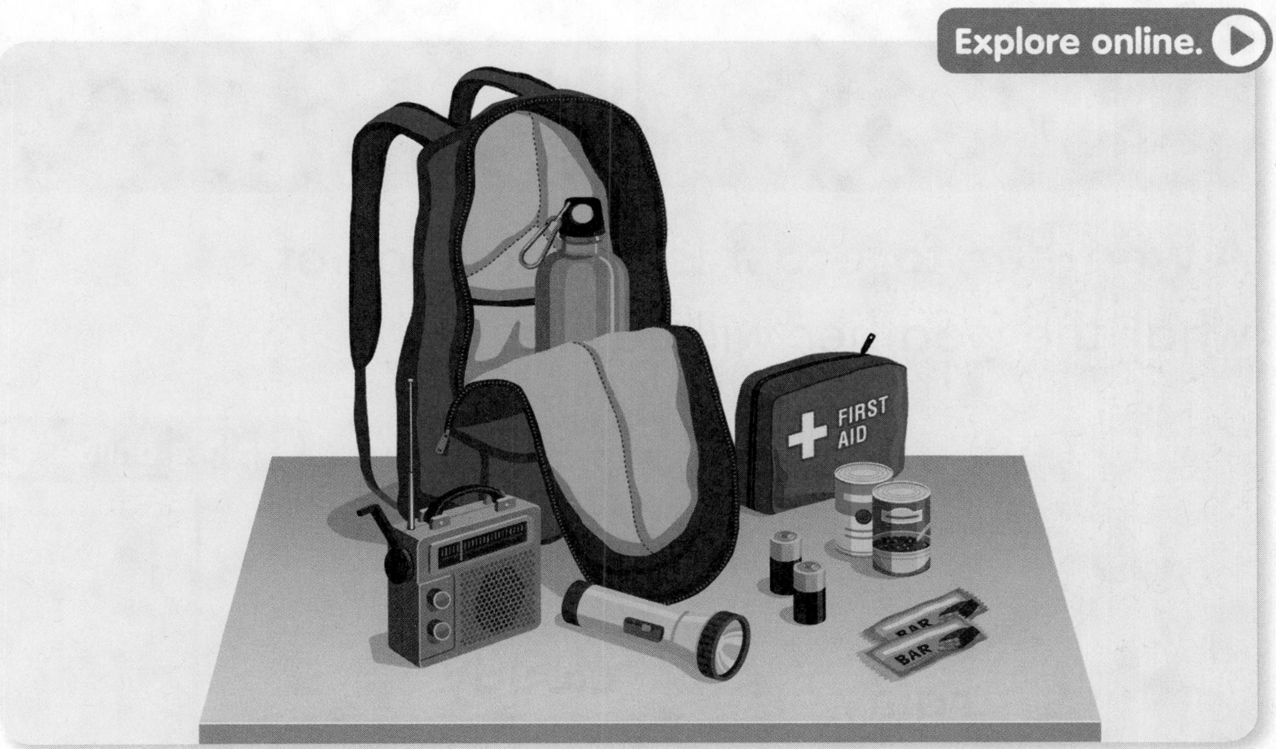

The things on the table will go into the bag. What do these things have in common?

Can You Explain It?

keep you safe

make you laugh

How would the things in the bag help you during severe weather? Circle your answer.

Weather Forecast

A **weather forecast** is a prediction of what the weather will be like.

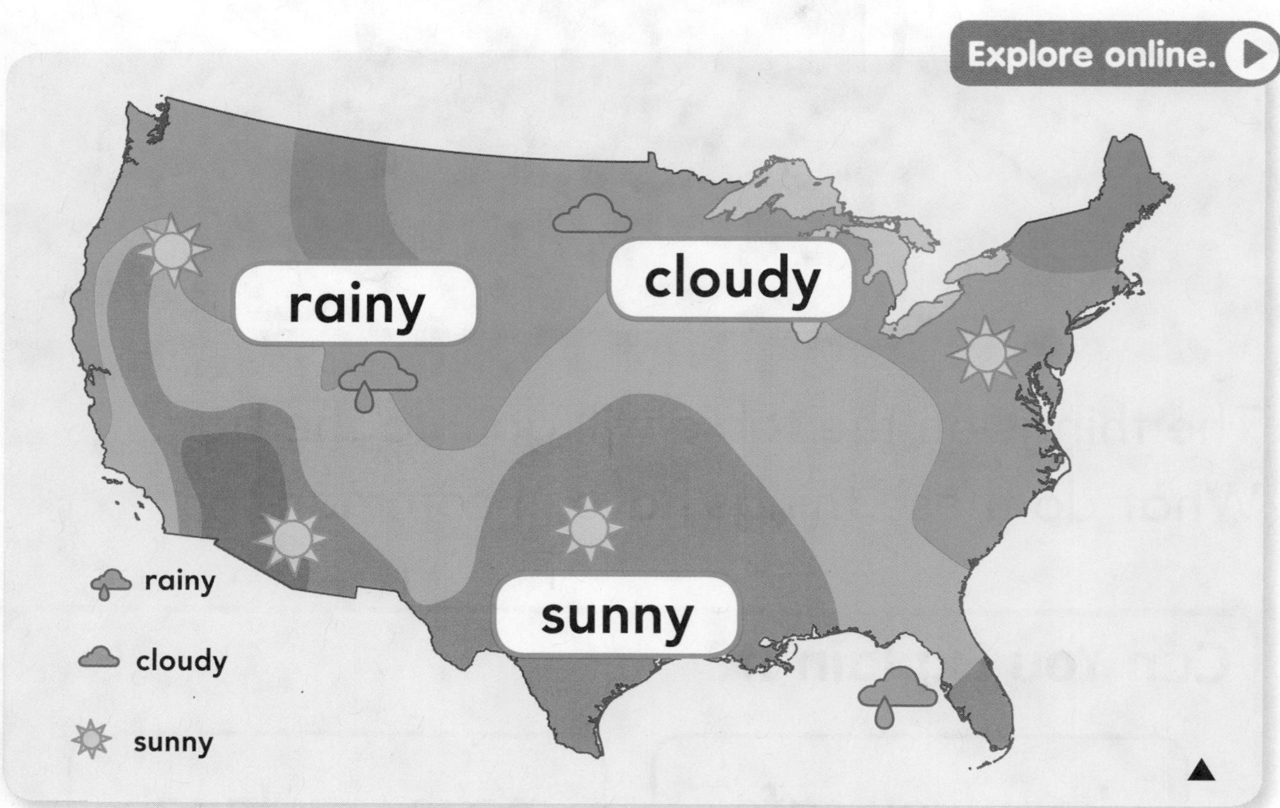

Weather maps show weather in many places.

• Circle the meteorologist giving a weather forecast. ▲ Draw a line under each symbol for rainy weather.

Do the Math!

Observe the kinds of weather in the months below. Count the sunny days in each month. Which month has more sunny days?

Counting Go to the online handbook for tips. 

Apply What You Know Read, Write, Share! ▲

Ask Questions Go to the online handbook for tips. 

• Circle the calendar that has more sunny days. ▲ Think of a question to ask a meteorologist. Use the Internet and books to find an answer. Share what you learn with others.

Prepare for Weather

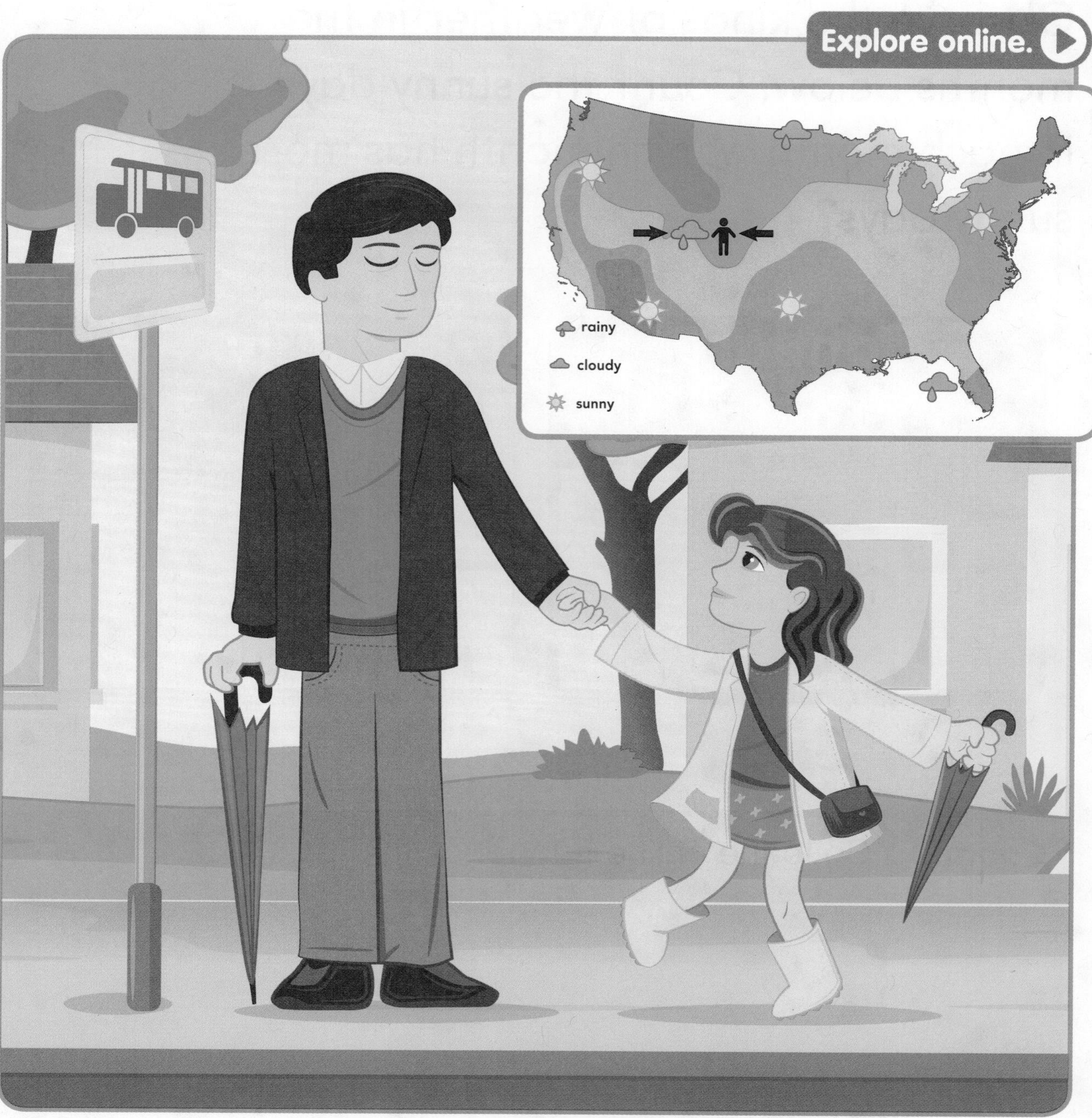

Maria wanted to know what the weather was going to be like. She looked at a weather map to find out.

Circle the part of the map that shows how Maria knew to take an umbrella.

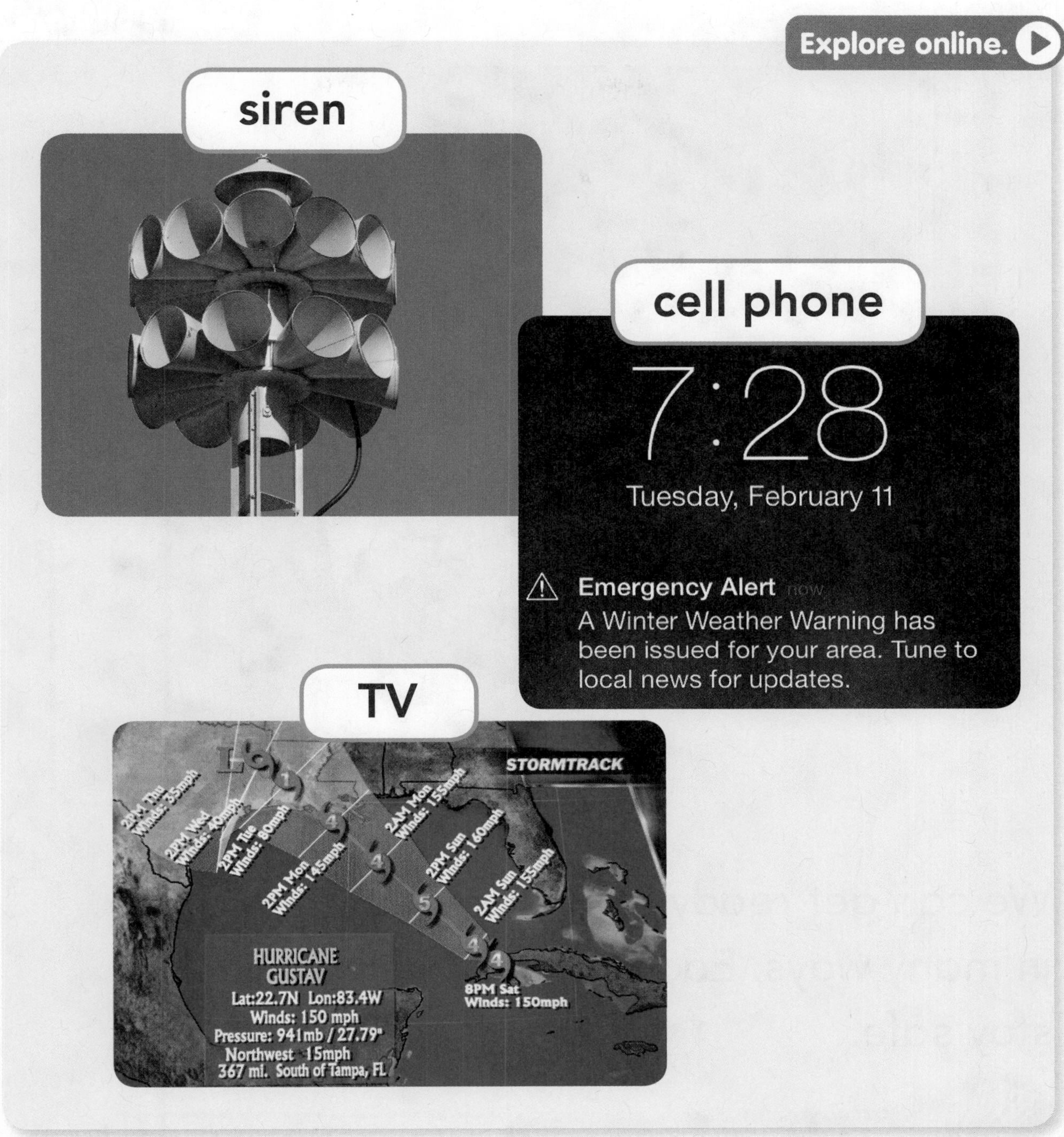

Weather warnings are sent in many ways. They help people get ready for severe weather.

Circle the severe weather warning for a hurricane.

Explore online.

We can get ready for severe weather in many ways. Each way can help us to stay safe.

Apply What You Know **Evidence Notebook** ▲

Influence of Technology Go to the online handbook for tips.

• Put an X on the picture that shows one way to protect your head during severe weather. ▲ How would it be different if we did not have technology to help forecast the weather? Use pictures and words as evidence to support your answer.

Name ______________________________

Hands-On Activity

Plan a Severe Weather Safety Kit

Explore online.

Materials

What do you need in a severe weather safety kit?

Step 1

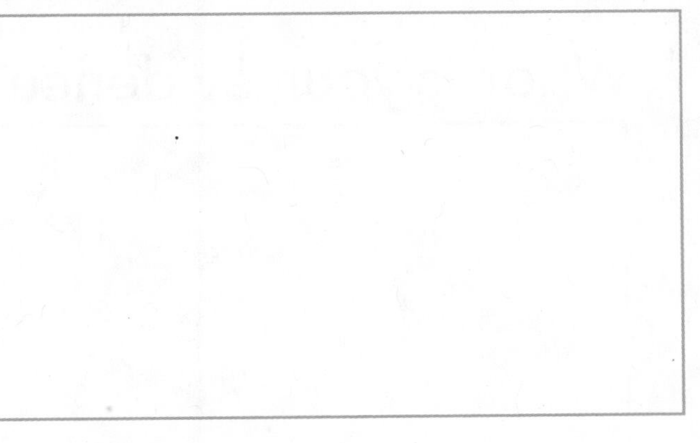

Ask questions about how weather safety kits would be different depending on the type of severe weather.

Step 2

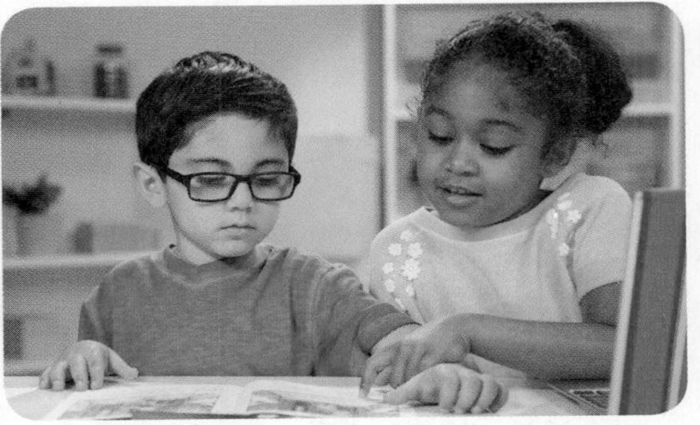

Choose a kind of severe weather. Find out what is needed to have prepared ahead of time.

Step 3

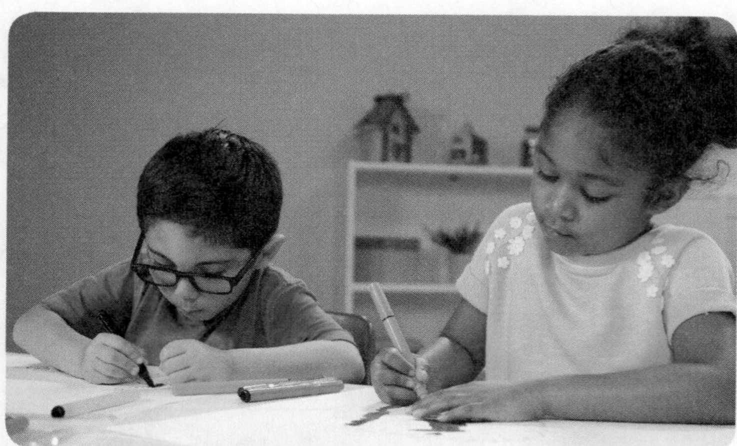

Draw to record what you find out.

Step 4

Make a plan for what would be included in your kit for this type of weather.

Make a claim.

What is your evidence?

Take It Further

Explore more online.

Amazing Animals

Tools Used to Predict Weather

Explore online.

Meteorologists use tools to collect weather information. They use the information to predict the weather.

Influence of Technology Go to the online handbook for tips.

Circle the satellite collecting weather information.

Weather Tools

Think about the pictures. Many tools are used to help look for weather patterns. Which of these pictures show a tool that is used to help predict the weather?

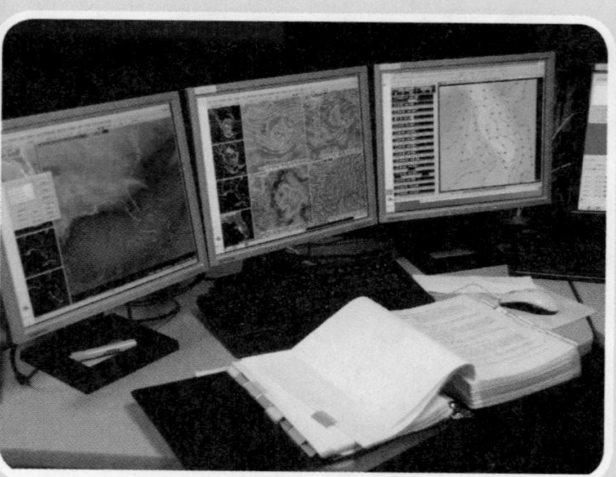

Circle the pictures that show a tool used to predict the weather.

Name ______________________

Lesson Check

Explore online.

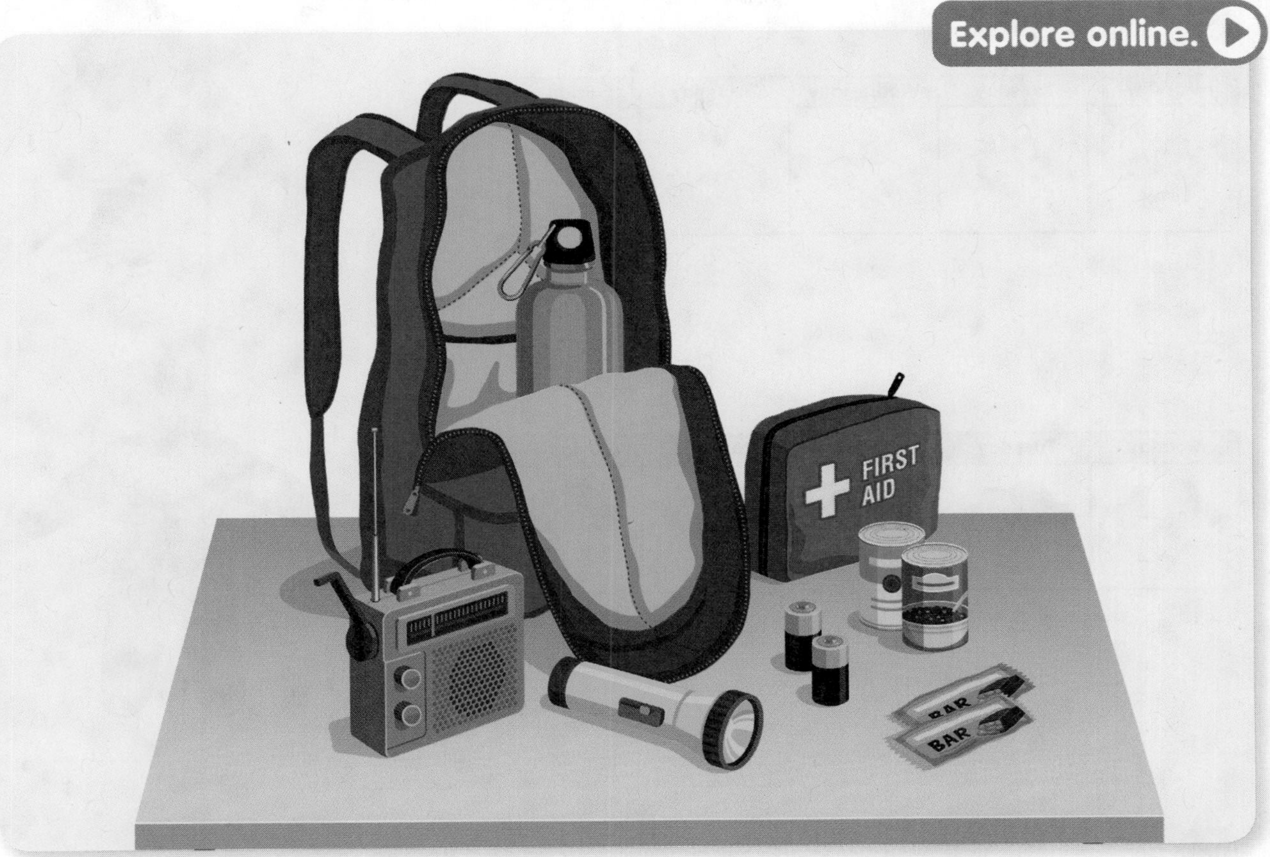

The things on the table will go into the bag. What do these things have in common?

Can You Explain It?

keep you safe

make you laugh

How would the things in the bag help you during severe weather? Circle your answer.

Self Check

Monday	Tuesday	Wednesday	Thursday	Friday

Monday	Tuesday	Wednesday	Thursday	Friday

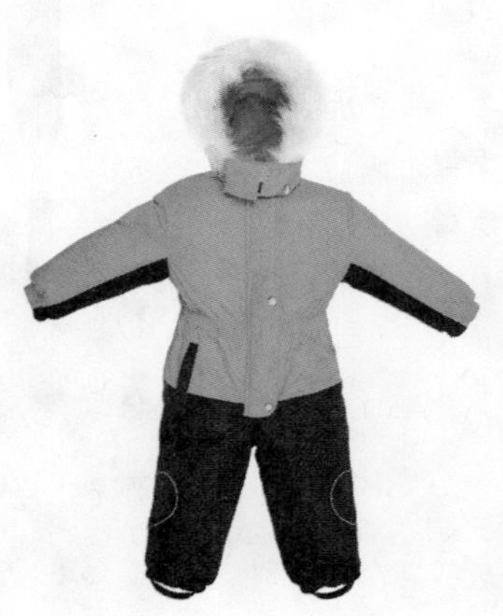

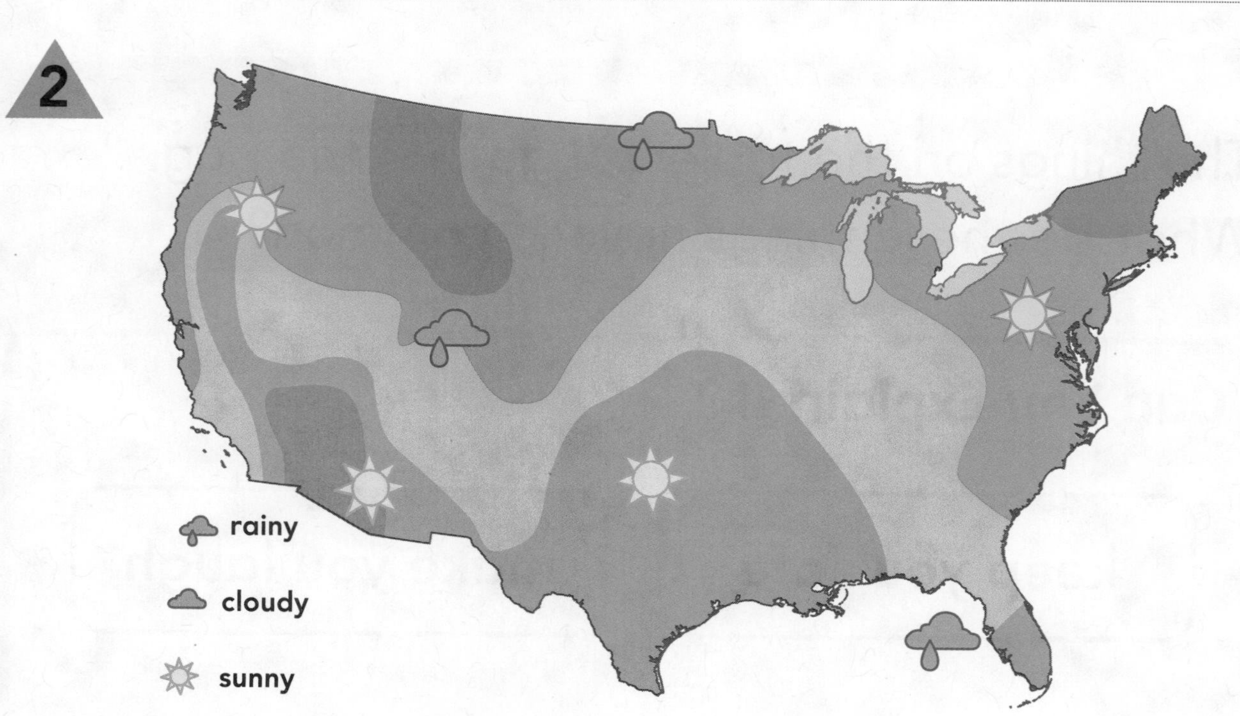

● Draw a line from the weather to the things that would be needed. ▲ Circle the places on the weather map that have sunny weather.

3

4

■ The weather forecast predicted rain and warm temperatures. Circle the pictures that show what Olivia should take to school. ✱ Circle the kind of weather when you might need a severe weather safety kit.

Unit 5 Performance Task
Changing Temperatures

Materials
- thermometer
- crayon

STEPS

Step 1
Place a thermometer outside.

Step 2
Read the temperature in the morning. Record the temperature.

Step 3
Read and record the temperature in the afternoon.

Step 4

Do this at the same time each morning and afternoon for four days.

Step 5

What pattern do you observe? Talk about it with others.

Check

_______ I read and recorded the temperature each morning.

_______ I read and recorded the temperature each afternoon.

_______ I did this for four days.

_______ I talked about the results with others.

Unit 5 Review

Name ____________________

1

3

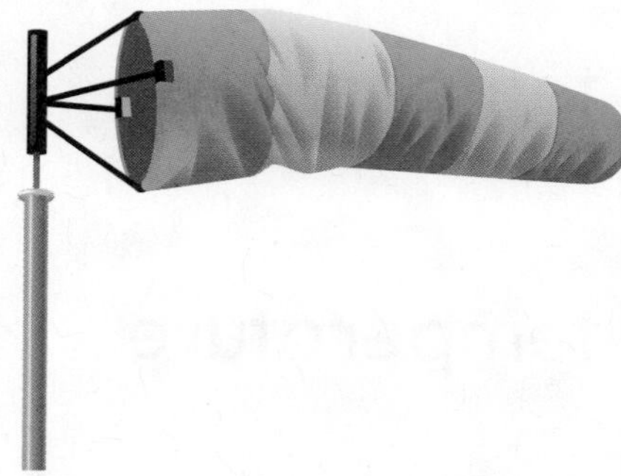
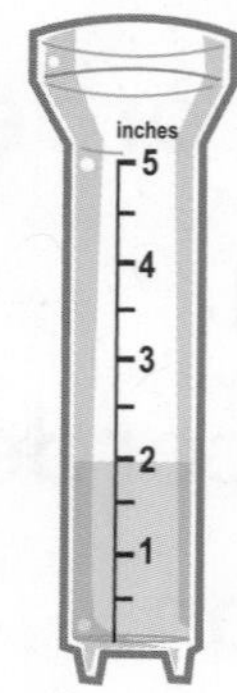

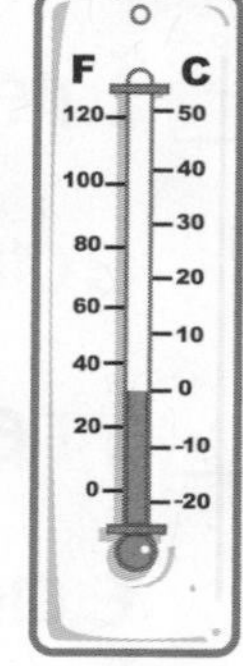

- ● Which pictures show a windy day? Circle the correct pictures.
- ▲ What would you wear in the warmest season? Circle the correct picture.
- ■ Which weather tool will help you know if it is cold enough to snow? Circle the correct picture.

Monday	Tuesday	Wednesday	Thursday	Friday

Monday	Tuesday	Wednesday	Thursday	Friday

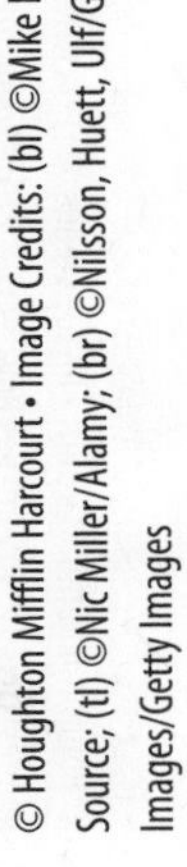

★ Which weather chart shows a pattern of rainy weather? Circle the correct chart.

● Which picture shows severe weather that is cold, windy and snowy? Circle the correct picture.

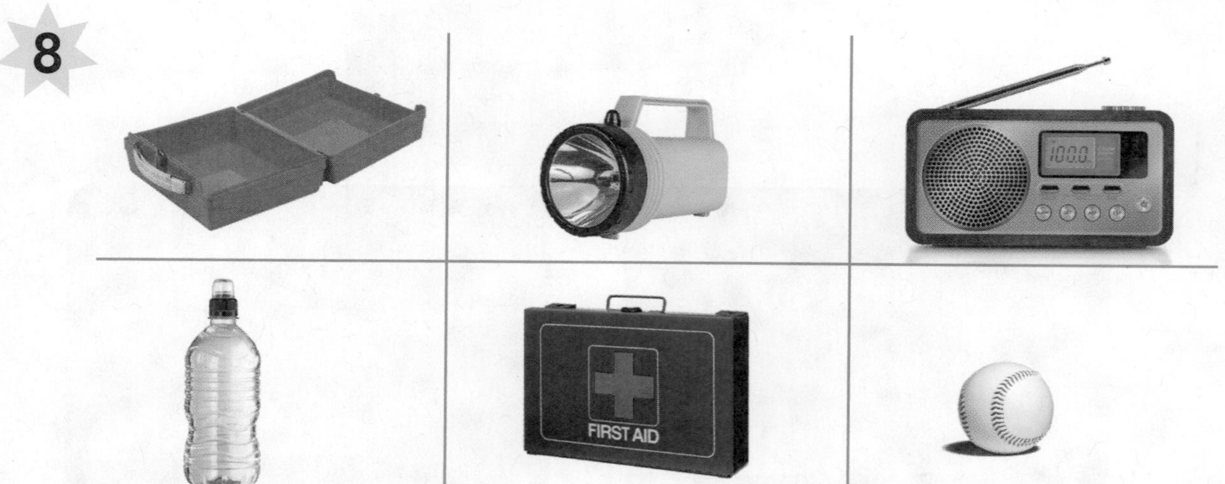

▲ Which pictures show severe weather? Circle the correct pictures.

■ Which pictures show things you might need in a thunderstorm? Circle the correct pictures.

✱ Which pictures show something that should be in a severe weather kit? Circle the correct pictures.

Unit 6
Earth's Resources

Unit Project • Reuse a Milk Carton

How can you reuse a milk carton? Investigate to find out.

Unit 6 At a Glance

Unit Vocabulary

natural resource anything people can use from nature (p. 248)

reduce use less (p. 266)

reuse use something again (p. 268)

recycle change something to make it into something new (p. 268)

Vocabulary Game • **Show the Word!**

Materials

- one set of word cards

How to Play

1. Make cards.
2. Place the cards face down.
3. One player picks a card and draws or acts out the word.
4. The other player guesses the word.

What Are Natural Resources?

By the End of This Lesson

I will be able to tell how people use natural resources.

Natural Resources

Many resources come from nature.
People use them in many ways.

Can You Explain It?

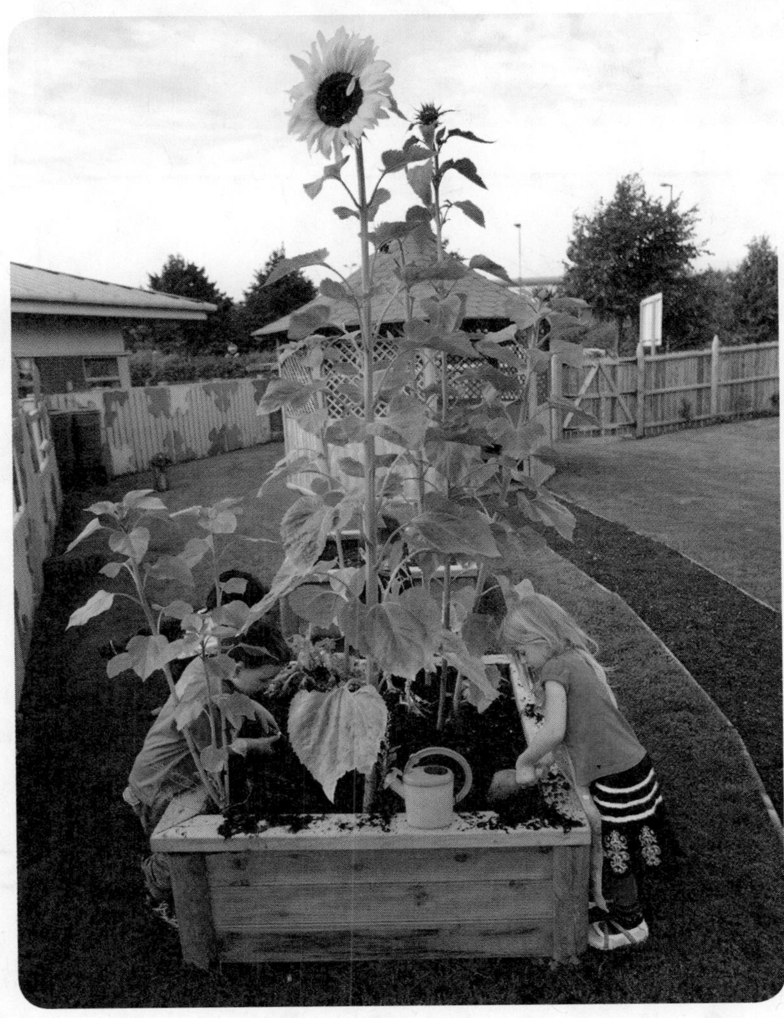

What resources come from nature? Circle all the natural resources.

Air

Air is a natural resource. It is part of a system. **Natural resources** are anything people can use from nature.

Systems and System Models Go to the online handbook for tips.

Color the thing the child is filling with air.

Explore online.

Air is all around us. Plants and animals need air. We use air in different ways.

Apply What You Know Do the Math! ▲

Know Number Sequence Go to the online handbook for tips.

● Circle the places where air is being used. ▲ How do you use air? One way is breathing. Count the number of breaths you take in 30 seconds.

Water

Explore online.

Water is a natural resource. We drink it and bathe with it. Water is part of a system.

Systems and System Models Go to the online handbook for tips.

Circle the people using water.

How is the natural resource water being used?

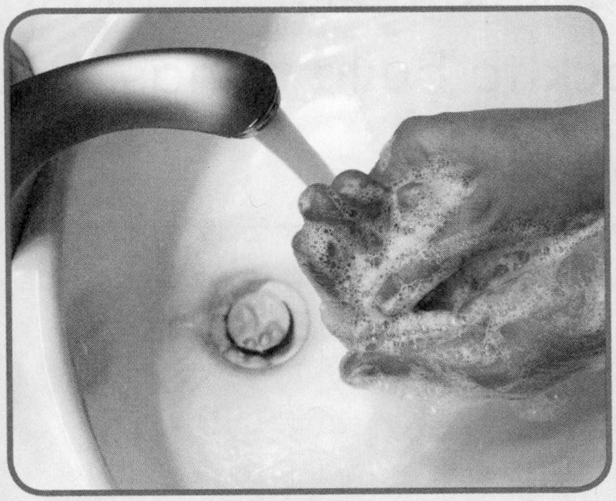

Apply What You Know Evidence Notebook ▲

Developing and Using Models Go to the online handbook for tips.

● Circle the pictures that show water being used. Draw a line under the people using air.
▲ Draw a picture of an animal using water. Use evidence to tell why it is important that animals use water.

Rock

Rock comes from the land. We use rock to build things. Rock is part of a system.

Draw

▲

Systems and System Models Go to the online handbook for tips.

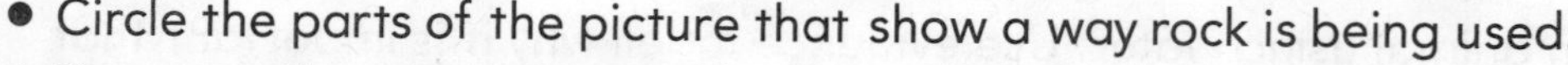

● Circle the parts of the picture that show a way rock is being used.

▲ Draw another way to use rock.

Explore online.

Apply What You Know Read, Write, Share! ▲

Use Visuals Go to the online handbook for tips.

● Color the places where rock is being used. ▲ Draw a picture of something made from rock. Share your drawing. Tell about how the rock was used.

Soil

Explore online.

Soil is a natural resource. We use it to grow plants. We use it to make bricks. Soil is part of a system.

- Circle the natural resource being used in each picture.

▲ Act out a way people use a natural resource.

Name ___________________________

Hands-On Activity

Clay Bricks

Explore online.

What can you make from clay?

Step 1

Fill each cube in the tray with clay.

Place the tray in a sunny, warm, dry place. Wait until the clay is dry.

Step 3

Take the clay out of the tray.

Step 4

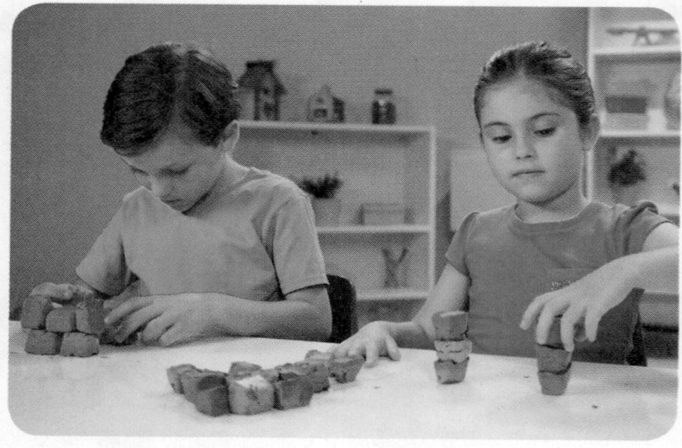

Use the clay bricks to build something.

Make a claim.

What is your evidence?

Take It Further

Explore more online.

Wind Energy

People in Science & Engineering • Theodore Roosevelt

Explore online.

Theodore Roosevelt was president of our country long ago. He wanted to protect our natural resources. He worked to help take care of them.

Circle the natural resources Theodore Roosevelt helped take care of.

Read, Write, Share!

Draw

Use Visuals Go to the online handbook for tips.

Developing and Using Models Go to the online handbook for tips.

Find out about a national park or forest in your state. Draw a model of it.

Name ___________________

Lesson Check

Many resources come from nature.
People use them in different ways.

Explore online.

Can You Explain It?

What resources come from nature? Circle all the natural resources.

Self Check

1

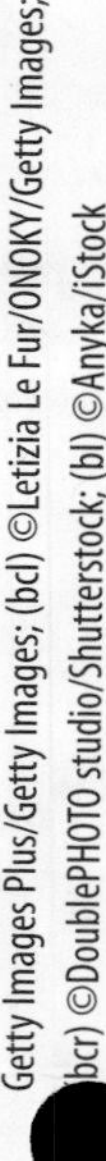

2

● Circle the natural resources. ▲ Circle the pictures of people using natural resources.

3

4

■ Circle the natural resources needed to grow tomatoes. ✱ Draw a line from the natural resource to the picture that shows how it is being used.

Lesson 2 Engineer It • How Can We Save Natural Resources?

By the End of This Lesson

I will be able to tell how people can help save natural resources.

Saving Natural Resources

There was too much trash being thrown away. How did the children help?

Explore online.

Can You Solve It?

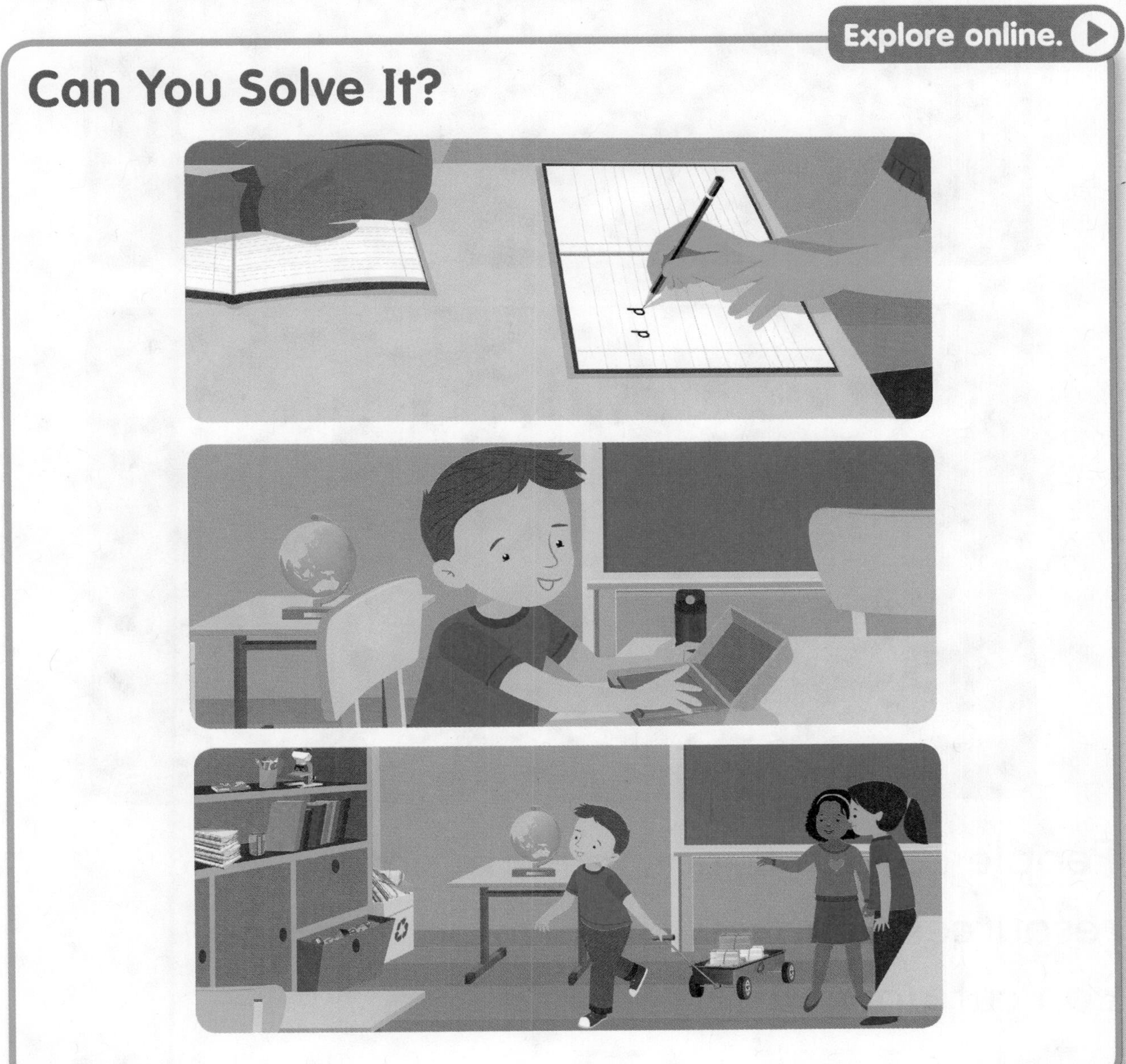

Circle the ways the children reduced the amount of trash being thrown away.

Harming Natural Resources

Explore online.

People can do things to harm natural resources. Smoke can harm air. People can cut down trees.

Cause and Effect Go to the online handbook for tips.

Circle the part of each picture that shows how a natural resource is being harmed.

How is the natural resource being harmed?

Cause and Effect Go to the online handbook for tips

Apply What You Know

• Draw a line to match the natural resource to the way it is being harmed. ▲ How can we harm natural resources? Work with a partner to make a list of all the ways a person can harm natural resources.

Reduce

Explore online.

People can help save natural resources. They can reduce what they use. **Reduce** means to use less.

Circle the part of each picture that shows a way someone is reducing the amount of natural resources being used.

How can natural resources be saved?

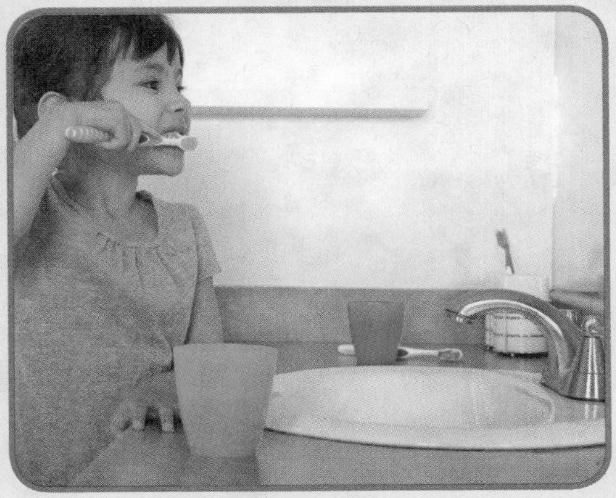

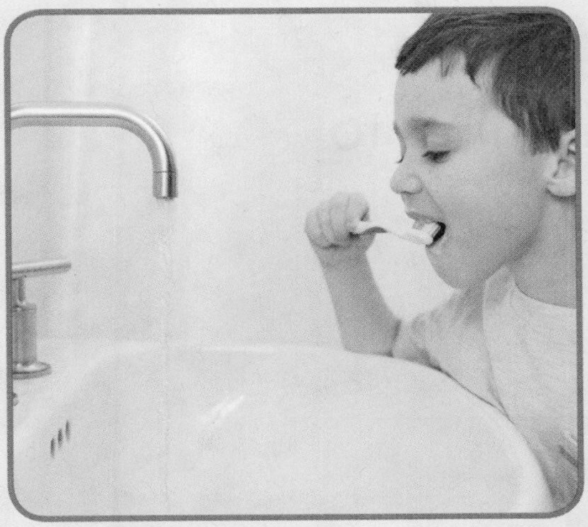

Apply What You Know Read, Write, Share!

Write to Inform Go to the online handbook for tips.

● Circle the children saving natural resources. ▲ Work with others to make a book about saving natural resources.

Reuse and Recycle

Explore online.

Reuse is to use something again.
Recycle is to change something to make it into something new.

Do the Math!

Count Go to the online handbook for tips.

Apply What You Know **Evidence Notebook** ■

- ● Circle the picture that shows something being reused.
- ▲ Look at the picture. How many things are being recycled? Write the number.
- ■ What can be recycled or reused at home? Write a plan. Use evidence.

Name ______________________

Hands-On Activity

Explore online.

Engineer It • Where Does Our Trash Go?

Materials

What happens to trash?

Step 1

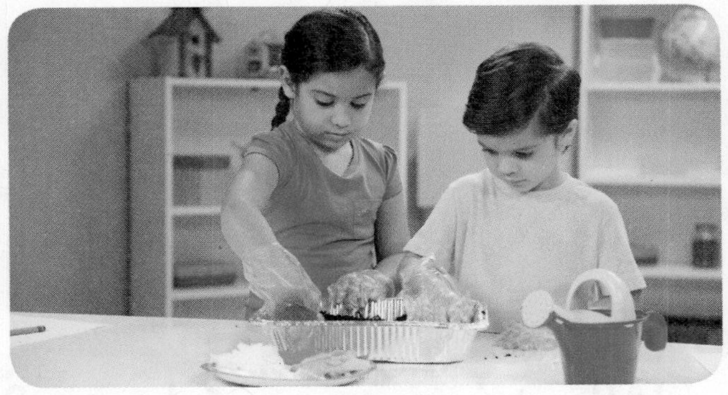

Bury the lettuce, napkin, and cup. Make sure it is covered with the soil.

Step 2

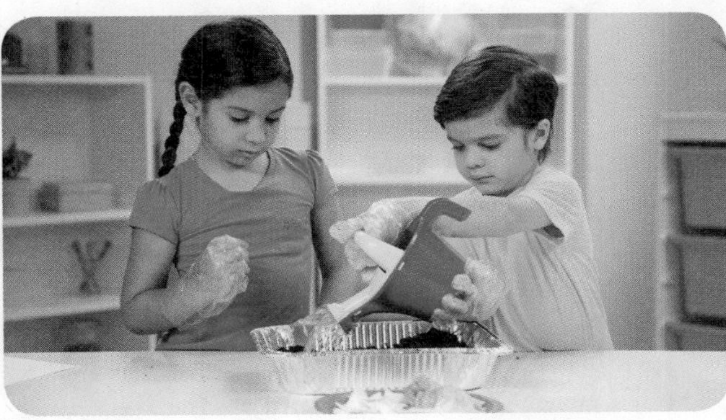

Water the soil every three days for two weeks.

Step 3

Dig up the lettuce, napkin, and foam cup. Tell why trash is harmful to the land.

Step 4

Draw a solution to help reduce the amount of trash that goes into a landfill.

Make a claim.

What is your evidence?

Take It Further

Explore more online.

Unusual Reusing

Careers in Science & Engineering • Recycling Center Operator

Explore online.

First, the operator loads the trash. The trash gets sorted. Then it is packed into squares.

Draw a line under the picture that shows the first step in recycling.

You can recycle most plastic, glass, and paper. Draw something made from plastic. Draw something made from glass. Draw something made from paper.

Name ______________________

Lesson Check

There was too much trash being thrown away. How did the children help?

Explore online.

Can You Solve It?

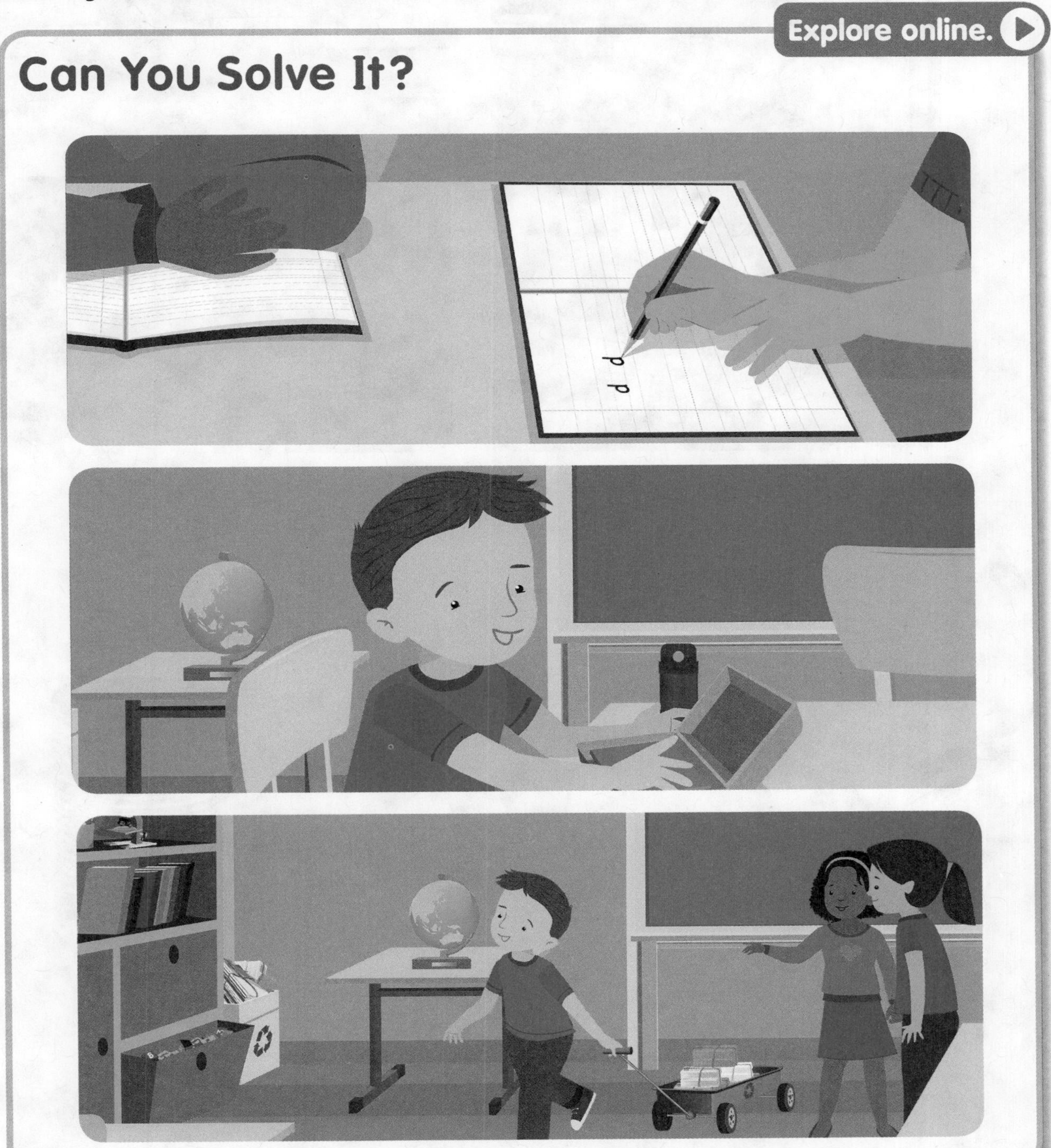

Circle the ways the children reduced the amount of trash being thrown away.

Self Check

1

• Circle the pictures of the girl saving natural resources. ▲ Circle the pictures of things that can be recycled to save natural resources.

3

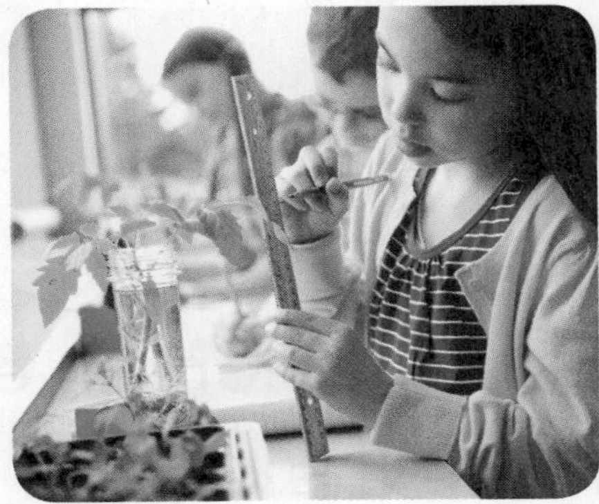

■ Circle the picture of someone helping to take care of natural resources. ✷ Draw a line from the natural resource to a way it is being used.

Unit 6 Performance Task

Natural Resources as a System

Materials

- marker
- soil
- water
- three small plants of the same type
- three plastic cups

STEPS

Step 1

Number the cups 1, 2, and 3.

Step 2

Place soil in Cups 1 and 2.
Do not place soil in Cup 3.

Step 3

Place a plant in each cup.
Place the cups in the sun.

Step 4
Water Cup 1 every other day for two weeks.

Step 5
Observe and describe. How are natural resources part of a system?

Check

_____ I put soil in two cups.
_____ I put plants in three cups.
_____ I watered the plant in Cup 1 every other day for two weeks.
_____ I observed the plants. Then I shared how natural resources are part of a system.

Unit 6 Review

Name ______________________

1

3

● Draw an X on each natural resource in the picture.

▲ Which picture shows a way people use soil as a natural resource? Circle the correct picture.

■ Which pictures show a child using air as a natural resource? Circle the correct pictures.

4

5

6

★ Which pictures show water being used as a natural resource? Circle the correct pictures.

● Which things can be recycled? Circle the correct pictures.

▲ Draw a line from the picture of pollution to the picture that shows what causes it.

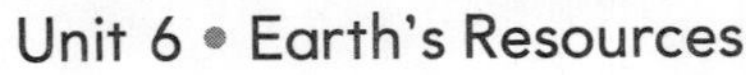

7

■ Which pictures show evidence of a way to reduce how we use a natural resource? Circle the correct pictures.

✱ Which pictures show a way to reuse a can? Circle the correct pictures.

Interactive Glossary

This Interactive Glossary will help you learn how to spell and define a vocabulary term. The Glossary will give you the meaning of the term. It will also show you a picture to help you understand what the term means.

Where you see [pencil], write your own words or draw your own picture to help you remember what the term means.

desert

A dry place. (p. 108)

design process

A set of five steps that engineers follow to solve problems. (p. 20)

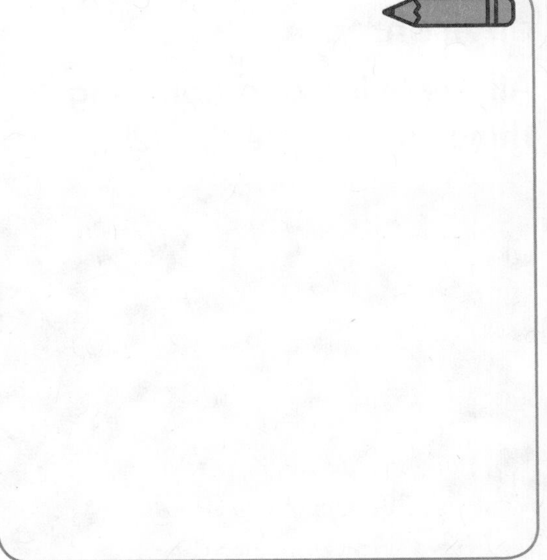

Interactive Glossary

direction

The path a moving object takes. (p. 47)

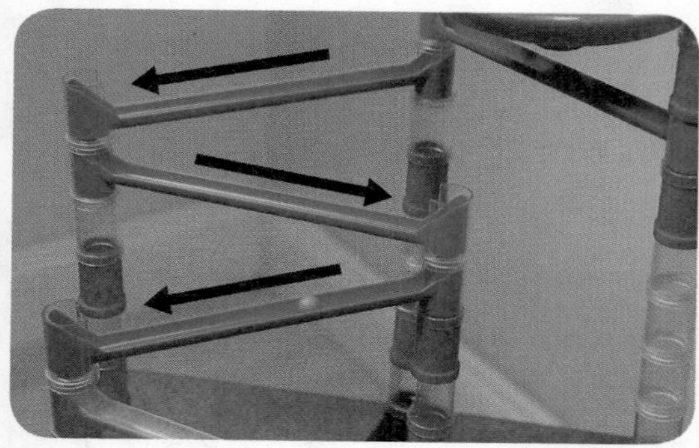

engineer

Someone who uses math and science to help solve problems. (p. 11)

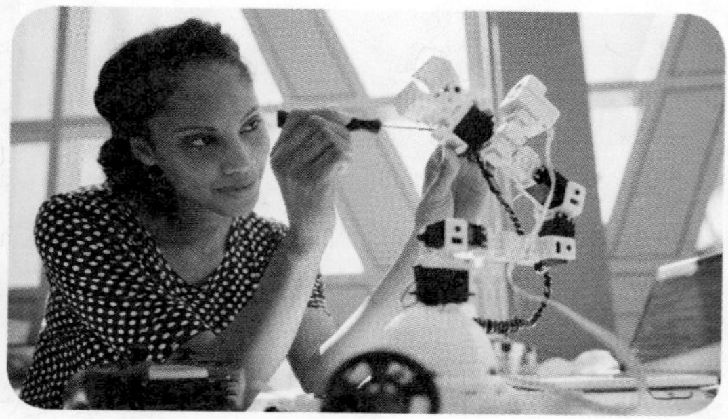

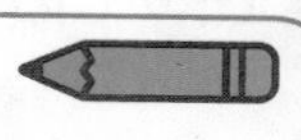

environment

All the living and nonliving things in a place. (p. 124)

force

A push or a pull that can make an object at rest move or an object in motion stop. (p. 56)

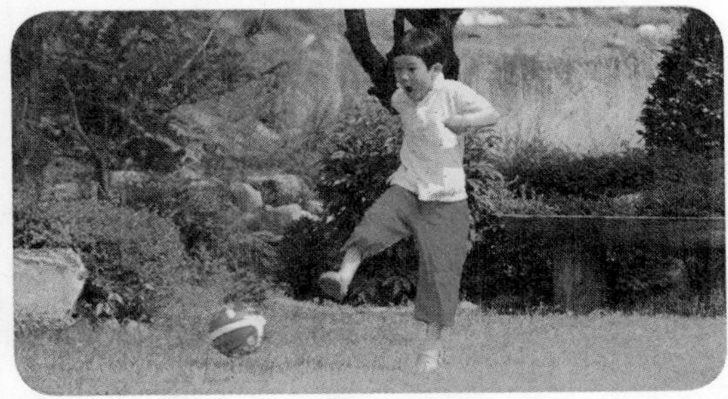

forest

Where many trees grow. (p. 110)

heat

Makes things warmer. (p. 150)

Interactive Glossary

light

Is what lets us see things. (p. 148)

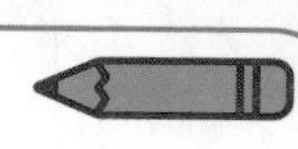

living things

Things that are alive. They need air,food, water, and space to live. (p. 76)

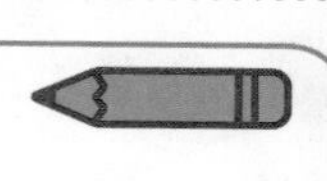

model

Something that shows what an object looks like and how it works. (p. 20)

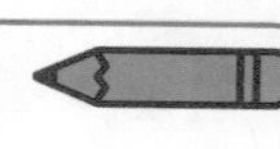

motion

The act of moving. (p. 42)

natural resource

Anything people can use from nature. (p. 248)

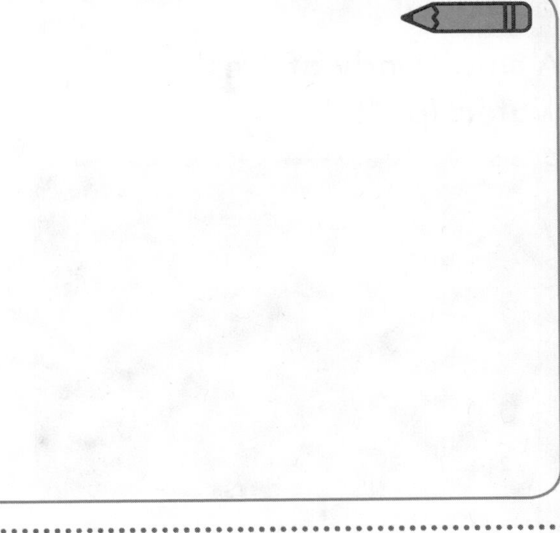

nonliving things

Things that are not alive. (p. 76)

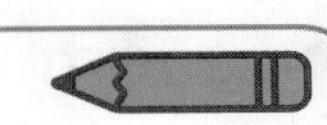

Interactive Glossary

ocean

A very large body of salt water. (p. 116)

pond

A small body of fresh water. (p. 114)

problem

Something that needs to be fixed or made better. (p. 6)

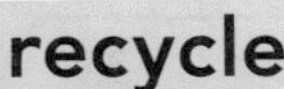

recycle

Change something to make it into something new. (p. 268)

reduce

Use less. (p. 266)

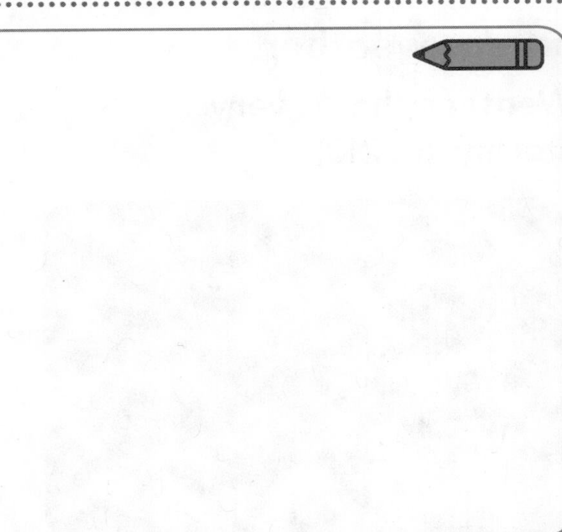

reuse

Use something again. (p. 268)

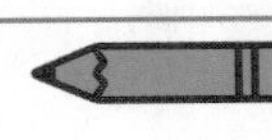

Interactive Glossary

season

A time of year that has a certain kind of weather. (p. 186)

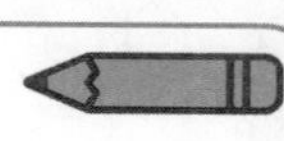

severe weather

Weather that is very stormy. (p. 210)

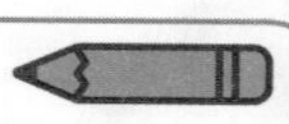

shade

Coolness caused by shelter from the sun's heat. (p. 160)

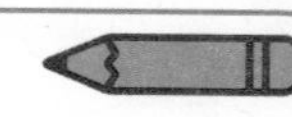

shelter

A place to live. (p. 94)

solution

Something that helps fix a problem. (p. 7)

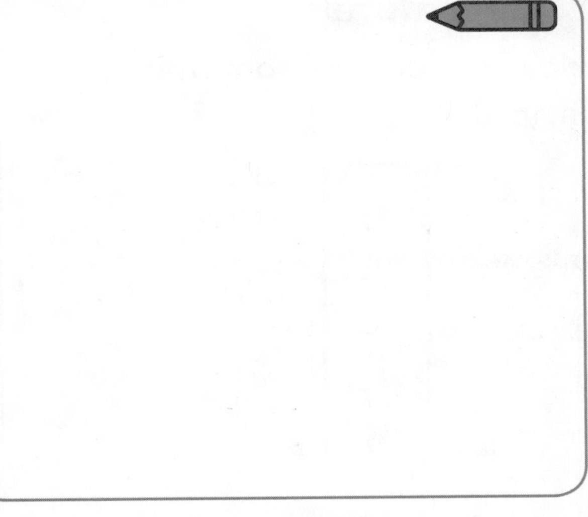

speed

How fast or slow something moves. (p. 44)

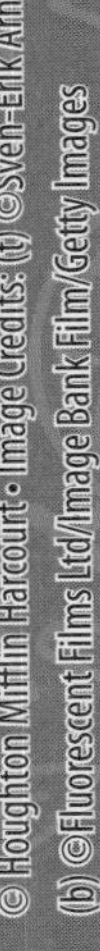

Interactive Glossary

technology

What engineers make and use to solve problems. (p. 12)

temperature

How hot or cold something is. (p. 196)

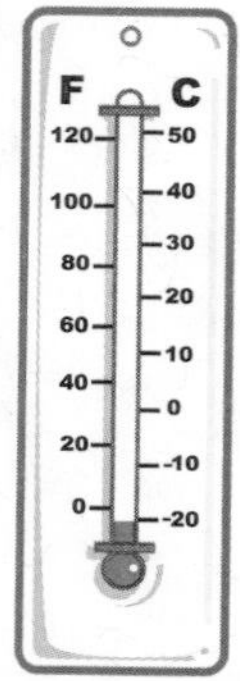

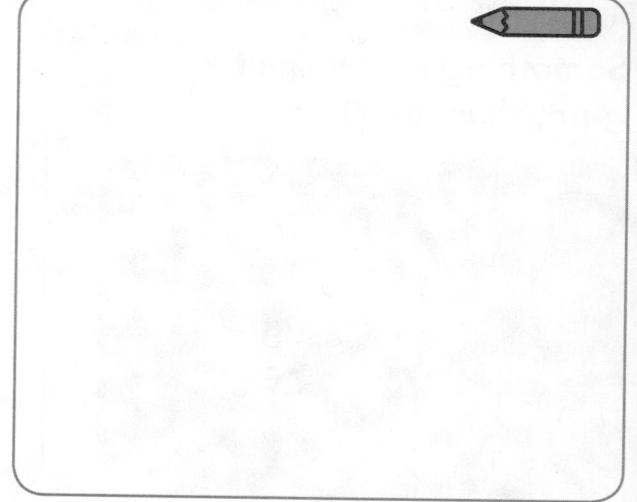

weather forecast

A prediction of what the weather will be like. (p. 226)

weather pattern

A change in weather that repeats. (p. 181)